Life Events

To Jo —

with blessings for every
event that life holds
for you o that
you hold for others,

Sarah Nun

Life Events

Mission and Ministry at Baptisms, Weddings and Funerals

Sandra Millar

CHURCH HOUSE PUBLISHING

Church House Publishing
Church House
Great Smith Street
London SW1P 3AZ

The opinions expressed in this book are those of the authors and do not necessarily reflect the official policy of the General Synod or the Archbishops' Council of the Church of England.

British Library Cataloguing in Publication Data

A catalogue record for this book is available
from the British Library

ISBN 978 1 78140 033 3

Typeset by Regent Typesetting
Printed and bound in Great Britain by
Ashford Colour Press

Contents

For Debbie, with whom
I've shared so many life events,
remembering our parents who
gave us love and made us laugh

Foreword

by the Right Reverend Robert Atwell, Chair of the Liturgical Commission

This highly anticipated book is the fruit of extensive research, analysis and discussion. It is full of insight about the ways in which ministers and congregations engage with people around 'life's key moments', be it the christening of a child, the wedding of a young couple, or the funeral of a dearly loved parent at the end of a long life. It challenges us to find imaginative ways of bringing to life our worship for those individuals who stand, quite literally, at the threshold of the Church looking in and seeking help, but who are often hesitant and not religiously articulate. The bereaved, for example, seek comfort and help in their hour of need, but invariably bring with them a clutch of inchoate beliefs with little or no Christian background to shape them.

For most of the last century, aspects of institutional religion have been in decline, at least in Britain and Western Europe. Life has been privatized, but paradoxically the search for meaning remains strong. In our fast-moving and apparently secular culture people may be allergic to dogma, but they crave the ether of spirituality. This generation is more interested in how something feels than whether or not it's true. Does it work for you? The sociologist Grace Davie has observed that today many people go to church to fulfil a particular rather than a general need in their life, and carry on going as long as it meets that need, but that's where their commitment ends. She says that as a generation we have moved 'from an understanding of religion as a form of obligation and towards an increasing emphasis on consumption'.[1]

These insights are confirmed by research funded by the Archbishops' Council into the conduct of 'occasional offices', to use their traditional generic title. In spite of a prevailing culture of hostility towards organized religion,

---

1 Grace Davie, 'From obligation to consumption: Understanding the patterns of religion in Northern Europe', *The Future of the Parish System*, ed. Steven Croft, Church House Publishing, 2006, p. 41.

she has discovered that people continue to seek out the Church at important moments in their lives because they value highly the things we do and what we have to offer. Interestingly, traditional forms and symbols continue to have great significance, even for those not otherwise engaged with church. In the case of baptism, for example, according to her research fewer than 10 per cent of families expressed an interest in services that were not 'traditional'. Part of the message of this book, therefore, is that the Church and her ministers should have greater *confidence* in what we offer at these important moments of life.

The research presented in this book underscores the importance of developing a good *relationship* with those who come to church seeking a baptism, a wedding, or to organize a funeral. In our increasingly not just de-churched but un-churched society, it is the quality of the relationship with the officiating minister that counts and the initial encounter invariably sets the tone for what follows. A good relationship is critical for establishing a longer-lasting pastoral link and Sandra Millar shares a series of creative ideas about how this relationship can be nurtured. This finding is hardly revolutionary, but it does need to be reinforced regularly. Ministry belongs to the whole people of God and she encourages us all to develop the *courage* for pastoral engagement at critical moments in life. In the varied circumstances of our lives and ministries, there are practical 'top tips' and 'special moments' to explore. In Part Three, a quotation from the Archbishop of York reminds us that 'the church [is] not the vicars or those who attend … we [all] come to that church as guests of Christ. Christ is the host. We are his guests.' Reflecting on his words, Sandra invites us to think about how we can best embody the unconditional, welcoming, loving-kindness of God manifested in Jesus Christ. The chapters that follow encourage us to have confidence in what we do as we worship, and suggest ways that we can make it the best it can be. Without warmth or welcome the liturgy soon feels tired and routine. Without an opportunity for reflection there is little chance of a deeper encounter. Matters will be made worse if those leading worship lose their way in the service or lard the liturgy with inappropriate mateyness. Worship that is slovenly conducted or lacklustre is unlikely to deepen anyone's spirituality.

Good worship is vital, not only because it is our duty and our joy to worship almighty God with all that we are and can offer, but also because it lies at the centre of all missional activity. Sadly, the experience of worship can be in sharp contrast to this ideal. But as Sandra points out, the good news of Jesus Christ can be shared again and again inexhaustibly; it is we who are a finite resource.

This last admission is part of the challenge she puts to us: telling the story of Jesus Christ through a blend of word, symbol, music and pastoral encounter is a great privilege and it is worth taking a fresh look at how we celebrate and mourn with the people who seek us out at life's key moments.

✠ Robert Exon

Part One

Mission at life's big moments

One of the strangest things about my life over the past few years is that I have become overfamiliar with the motorway network of England and its service stations. I could probably have it as my specialist subject on *Mastermind*. I even have a favourite motorway. That happens to be the M6 toll road, which bypasses Birmingham and is worth every penny of the fee for the sheer joy of driving on 27 miles of virtually empty road.

One day I was on this particular motorway and decided to stop at the Norton Canes services. As I purchased my coffee I chatted to the young woman serving me. I probably said something inane about how busy the service area seemed to be, and then she said, with a tinge of pride and a slight squaring of her shoulders, 'Well, this is the busiest Costa in the world, you know.' I smiled politely, while thinking to myself that this was unlikely. How could what seems like the world's quietest motorway possibly host the world's busiest Costa? A few months later I was regaling a colleague with this story, and before I had even finished telling it, he was googling the answer. In an incredulous voice, he looked up and said, 'It is the world's busiest Costa by volume of sales' (see www.hospitalityand cateringnews.com).

This story may seem a random way to introduce a book about mission and ministry at life's key moments. But it is a reminder that sometimes brief passing contact with people can add up to something that has real significance. For some customers a passing visit will be a first contact with that product, while for others it will be part of their everyday life. But each and every person is part of the story.

1

What is this book about?

Even in a culture where organized religion is of decreasing importance for many people, the one place they may still encounter the story of God and God's people is when a significant 'life event' happens. This is the moment when they make that 'passing contact' that may become part of their faith story and their relationship with God and God's people.

For generations, the Church of England has been meeting people at key moments on life's journey, particularly at the beginning of life, in marriage, and at the end when someone we know and love dies. Despite the fact that the numbers have declined over the past decades, there are still thousands of people each week who are in touch with the Church of England at one of these key moments, whether at the heart of the event or in attendance to support others.

This book is about the ordinary, often unsung work that goes on week in, week out in parishes throughout England as the Church undertakes what have traditionally been known as the 'occasional offices', as people are buried, married and celebrate new beginnings. It draws on existing good practice and the findings of extensive targeted research with those who still choose to contact the Church to help them celebrate or commemorate a key life event.

It is for all those who are involved with meeting people at these key life events, whether as lay support teams, congregation, clergy or readers, through leading services, welcome or prayer. The book shares the insights and key messages that have emerged from research so that parishes can reflect on their own experience. Throughout there are quotes from the research participants, enabling us to listen to the voices of those we meet at life's key moments. The book also offers practical ideas that will help parishes to make the most of the opportunities for contact that come through the baptism of a child, weddings and funerals, and explores ways in which such contact might contribute to church growth. Each section concludes with practical actions and key steps, and the last section contains useful information about how to access print and online resources that will support this vital ministry in every parish.

This book will be a reminder for those who have attended a presentation on the key insights emerging from the research, and will be an opportunity for those who missed such an event to engage with the research and resources.

This book is not the end of the work that the national Church of England is doing to support ministry around weddings, funerals and the baptism of a child. It is a tool to help as many parishes and people as possible discover fresh ideas and vision about how these particular moments can be part of sharing the good news of God's love revealed in Jesus Christ. The work continues with the development of new resources, fresh ideas and ongoing research, for caring for people in times of celebration and times of sadness is at the heart of much of parish life in the Church of England.

Finding your way round the book

- This book is in five parts. This section, Part One, explores the background, purpose and process behind the 'Life Events' work.

- Part Two looks at ministry around the time of birth, and how we can welcome families through baptism.

- Part Three considers wedding ministry and the journey that couples who choose a church wedding might make with us.

- Part Four examines funeral ministry, looking at how we talk about death and dying as well as the funeral service and bereavement care.

- Part Five includes an Afterword on current and future plans for the Life Events work, a resources list and an overview of the Life Events websites.

The story so far: From 'projects' to 'Life Events'

In 2008 there was a significant change in the law around marriage with the introduction of the Marriage Measure 2008, which established the principle of 'qualifying connection', opening up the possibility of a church wedding to thousands of couples for whom it might otherwise have been difficult if not impossible. Against this background, the Archbishops' Council decided to invest in research to understand just what couples really felt about church weddings, what made them choose to marry there and what stopped them. This led to the development of the Weddings Project, which reflected on the research findings and disseminated these to clergy nationwide through training and resources. The aim was to highlight good practice and to focus on ways in which the Church could improve in its ministry and mission to wedding couples and their friends and families, through responding to the research with couples themselves.

The Weddings Project made a huge impact, both through its method of working and in the way that the insights were presented throughout the Church to both encourage and challenge clergy to think differently. In 2012, the Archbishops' Council decided to invest further to see if there were fresh insights to be found by researching ministry around the time of birth and the time of death.

I was appointed as Head of the Life Events projects in 2013, with a brief to develop this work, building on the model that had been used for the work around weddings and identifying the possibilities for resourcing and supporting local churches. In this role, I support and encourage churches in this amazing work of building relationships, serving people in need and sharing the good news of the gospel. I come from a background in retail marketing, academic research, mission, children and families work and parish ministry, and lead a core team of five people, most of whom are freelance specialists. The team bring many skills including marketing expertise, web knowledge, social media skills and theological insights. We have drawn on the insights of market research professionals, designers, web developers and communicators to develop resources that will equip the Church to continue this important ministry into the twenty-first century. Alongside the core team, we also created a working group for each life event, consisting of clergy, lay people and diocesan specialists from a range of parish contexts. These groups were very important in ensuring that the ideas that developed were grounded in pastoral realities.

When this work first began in 2008 it was known as 'Projects and Developments', a title that was appropriate for work that was very new in the Church of England. However, we are now known as the 'Life Events Team', a change that happened in 2017 to reflect the acceptance that work around funerals, baptisms and weddings is ongoing for the Church of England, part of who we are and what we do. It also reflects an emphasis on those who come to us for some of the most important and memorable moments in their lives. We still have 'projects' as we develop new resources and tools to help parishes, but this small change in terminology represents a big turning point for this work.

The research process

The insights and resources that have emerged over the past decade, since the beginning of the work around weddings, are all rooted in deep, professional research. We have worked with leading research agencies including the Henley Centre, ESRO and others to identify the right research strategy and questions, and it is they who have conducted the research on our behalf. Different agencies worked on each of the big life events as we explored the real experiences and expectations of those who come to us for one of those events. Throughout this book the voices of those who shared their experiences with us can be heard: quotations directly from the research appear throughout and some are unattributed.

Weddings. The research for the original Weddings Project involved talking with 2,000 people about their attitudes to marriage, using surveys at national wedding shows. A robust sample of couples was also interviewed in depth, talking about their experiences and expectations of a church wedding, and we held focus groups with clergy in two different dioceses. Full details of this process can be found in Gillian Oliver, *The Church Weddings Handbook* (CHP, 2012).

The baptism of a child under 12. The core research involved interviews with 1,000 parents of children under two who had been baptized in the last four years, and then a series of in-depth interviews supported by a Facebook research group. We also held focus groups with parents who had chosen not to have a child baptized, talked with 300 clergy across every deanery in two dioceses, and used internet surveys with a further 2,000 people to understand some of the language that is used by parents and families.

Funerals. We used a leading social research agency to conduct in-depth interviews with those who had recently organized a funeral for an older relative; we also interviewed the CEOs of 30 leading organizations involved in death, dying and funerals, and did two surveys of funeral directors. We talked to clergy and Readers in focus groups and sent a questionnaire to retired clergy as well.

The data that emerged from the different phases and types of research has been carefully considered and analysed by researchers from beyond the Church of

England, who have brought their questions and insights into the discussions. We then worked with design agencies, writers and web developers to create resources and practical tools to help parishes. We invited 150 parishes across four dioceses to a 24-hour conference on baptism ministry and a further 150 parishes across four dioceses to a 24-hour conference on funeral ministry. These clergy were then invited to use the insights and the resources for 12 months, during which time we met with them in focus groups, listened to their thoughts online and sent two surveys to help us assess usefulness and impact.

After all that, we launched the resources to the wider Church of England through a series of national, regional and diocesan day conferences. By late 2017, 35 dioceses had either held or booked a conference about funeral ministry, and a further 31 around baptism ministry. In addition, 30 dioceses took part in the Weddings Project before 2012.

It is this research process that lies at the heart of the findings of this book, ensuring that there are practical, effective steps that can be taken at a local level.

Biblical reflection: Sowing seeds

In a culture in which many people may have little or no contact with the Church on a regular basis, we began to reflect on the potential significance of ministry at key life events (or the 'occasional offices'), seeking ways to encourage those we meet on their lifelong journey. Alongside the external research process, we spent some time thinking and praying and looking at biblical models for mission and evangelism. The team were drawn to reflect on the parable of the sower (Matthew 13.1–19) and were reminded by a vicar from a farming background that for many of Jesus' first-century listeners this story would have raised at the very least a wry smile if not an outright laugh. It is often a challenge for us to remember that as a good storyteller Jesus would have used humour to engage the audience, sometimes to make them laugh at themselves, at others to draw attention to something new and challenging. Most of Jesus' original listeners would have been sowing seed, if not to feed the Romans then to feed their own kinship group, and no sensible farmer would ever have just gone out to sow some seed in a careless, reckless manner, letting it fall in all kinds of different places. This is what would have made them smile, for seed costs money; it is a limited resource and therefore has to be used wisely and carefully.

While parables work on many levels, often speaking to us in different ways at different stages of our lives, there is a sense in this parable that the farmer may be saying something to us about the way in which God sows the seed of God's love in the world. This idea was supported when I listened to the theologian Ann Morisy talking about God's economy of abundance at a diocesan clergy conference. She suggests that while as citizens of twenty-first-century Europe we live in an economy built on the principle of scarcity (just as the citizens of first-century Palestine did), God's economy is fundamentally different. The principle of scarcity means that every human resource we have runs out – and our economy is built around that, so things that are more abundant tend to be cheaper, and those that are hard to find are more expensive. But God's economy is built on abundance – the resources that can never run out.

The good news of God's love revealed in Jesus Christ can be told and retold and told again – it will never be exhausted! We can share the good news at weddings, funerals, baptism of children, with Sunday congregations, at carol concerts, in the street, and there will always be a fresh supply (although we our-selves are a finite resource!).

The opportunities to show God's love and to share the good news of Jesus Christ at life events are immense. It is about mission, it is about service and it is also about evangelism, as each and every encounter with the good news draws people close to Jesus.

There is also a sense in which ministry at life events can reach those who would not feel able to access this in any other way. One of the requirements of the Hebrew law as outlined in Leviticus and Deuteronomy is an instruction that fields should not be harvested completely; there should always be some crops left at the edges so that the poorest and most destitute could come close and find food (Leviticus 19.9ff.). Ministry around life events is one way in which those who are on the margins can draw close to the good news of God's love. Some-times this is literally those who are on the edge of our society, at others it may be those who feel unable to access church and faith in any other way.

The three big purposes

We reflected on further insights from Scripture in relation to each of the big life moments, and those thoughts are shared in each section. Alongside our reflection on the generous, abundant, unconditional love of God we had three core purposes, which have underpinned this work right from the inception of the Wedding Project. These purposes emerged from the tasks that the Archbishops' Council gave to the Weddings Project team:

- To **attract** more weddings in church.
- To **build** public awareness of the Church's enthusiasm for marriage through proactive media, weddings shows and online.
- To **care** for couples and guests so well that more of them want to stick with the Church after the day (Gillian Oliver, *The Church Weddings Handbook*, p. 6).

It is these three words – **attract, build, care** – that have shaped everything we do, and underpin all the thinking and the practical resources in this book. The next section explores each of these purposes in more detail, looking at how they have informed thinking and development.

Attract – choosing church at life-changing moments

Attracting people is not just about encouraging people to choose the Church of England for a ceremony to mark one of life's key events, although the ceremony is important as people mark significant 'rites of passage'. Each of these key life moments generates big thoughts, big feelings and often big questions. When we face life changes, beyond the detail of organizing the event to mark the change, feelings about identity, self-worth, the meaning of life and death, responsibility, commitment, love and many other issues are all swirling around. Market researchers in the retail world know that these life stages will often result in major changes in behaviours and choices:

People's buying habits are more likely to change when they go through a major life event. (Charles Duhigg, *The Power of Habit*, p. 192)

In his book *Something More*, John Pritchard identifies the potential of significant life events to cause change and disruption to long-held behaviours and beliefs:

Without realizing it a thin veneer of concrete has probably settled over our way of life, our habits, beliefs and values. It then needs some fairly major event to disrupt those patterns and to break up the concrete so that something new can come through. Often this is the arrival of a child, but it could be a final decision to get married, or, sadly, it could be an accident or tragic death. (p. 92)

One of the places that people can bring all those thoughts, feelings and questions is their local Church of England, where we have journeyed with people through life's big events not just for a decade or two but for generation after generation. The purpose of reflecting and researching on our ministry at life's key moments is not about getting people to have a service but about showing them the love of God revealed in Jesus Christ.

Build – understanding them and us

The second core purpose is about building understanding. At one level, much of the work we have done is about helping those who come to the Church for a ceremony to mark a significant event to understand who we are and what we offer. We no longer live in a culture that is just one or two generations post-church, but one in which it might be five or six generations since anyone was regularly involved with church. For many people the 'pointy building down the street' is a complete mystery. In some communities, new housing and development means that the church building is no longer at the heart of the residential community but pushed out to the edges. I remember driving up and down and round and round a large village looking for the church. Eventually I stopped a street cleaner, thinking that he was bound to know. I wound down the window and asked my question. He looked worried and said, 'There you have me. I've never been asked that before.' He had no idea. And when I eventually found it I wasn't surprised, as the church was now remote from the busy centre of the village.

In recent years many high street businesses that were traditionally hidden from view have become more transparent. As one vicar put it: 'There used to be three places in the street that you couldn't see into: the betting shop, the sex shop and the church. Two of those have changed.'

Betting shops began to change in the 1980s and now it is easy to see what happens within; they have large glass windows and a quick glance in from the street will show comfortable seats as well as the paraphernalia of the business. And, of course, many a shopping mall will have an Ann Summers shop uninhibitedly displaying things that a generation or two ago would definitely have been behind closed doors!

By contrast, it is not always easy to see inside a church. Stained-glass windows are beautiful once you are on the inside, but from the outside they may look remarkably like windows with bars on. While an ancient wooden door with its heavy locks is a symbol of the enduring nature of the building, it may look very forbidding. What goes on in the building, what it offers and who can access it, is no longer commonly known. Noticeboards may be out of date or use so much church jargon that only those who are already actively involved would understand. Terms such as 'Sung Eucharist' or 'vestry hour' are not familiar to most people. So part of the work that has developed around weddings, funerals and baptisms is aimed at helping people discover more of who we are and what we offer, letting them know what and who to ask and what they might expect when they get inside.

But building understanding is not just about what 'they' (i.e. those who don't normally come to church) don't know. It is also about building understanding within the Church. The Church of England, like many churches, is really good at knowing what people in a local community need, but all too often without ever asking them! Time and again we make plans and create new schemes based on our assumptions about the needs and thoughts of those around us. I remember when I worked as Children and Families Officer in the Diocese of Gloucester going to visit lovely village parishes where a group had asked for help in setting up an after-school club for the children. After a few questions about how many children were in the village, it slowly emerged that there were probably only about 14 children in total and 11 of them went to boarding school! It just might be that a bit of research would uncover some very different needs in that particular place.

The research base of the Life Events work helps us to build our understanding of what motivates those who come to us at one of life's key moments. It helps us discover what people may really be thinking and feeling, what their expectations are and what they actually experience when they meet with us through the occasional offices. Sometimes this research takes us by surprise, at others it confirms our own experiences and insights, but it is the driver for all that has been developed to help the Church as it engages with people.

Care – doing things well

The third core purpose is about caring – or doing what we do in such a way that we draw people onwards into a lifetime journey of discovering all that it means to be a follower of Jesus Christ. It is about finding out and implementing those things that enable people to 'come back after' and stick with church. As the work has developed and continued it has also emerged that caring is about consistent good practice within a parish, across deaneries and a diocese and ultimately throughout the Church of England. It is about caring that those who visit a church to arrange having their banns read get the same kind of welcome as they do in a different church where they go to light a candle as they remember a grandparent who recently died.

Researchers into consumer behaviour and customer loyalty know the importance of good experiences and good memories, particularly at the first point of contact.

> *The experiences we remember are defined by change. Experiences that are new, novel or personally meaningful provide emotional peaks in a stream of experience. Finally, our remembering self likes endings, how experiences conclude, the big finish.* (KPMG, 'Making Memories')

The 'Making Memories' report looks at top-performing firms and how they ensure that customers have enough good experiences so that future choice is made on the basis of 'anticipated memories', built on those good moments. Organizations as diverse as John Lewis, Lush, Emirates and First Direct bank all comment on how they focus on giving people a positive memory that goes beyond expectations, building an emotional connection that outlasts the day. We may not have the same commercial intent or use the same business language, but the desire to do things so well that people return is essentially similar. Attracting, building, caring – all three purposes underpin the broader purpose of opening up the opportunities of witnessing to God's welcome, sharing the good news of Jesus Christ and enabling people to share the journey of faith, discovering all the 'fullness of life' (John 10.10) promised in Jesus.

There are so many people who have had contact with the Church of England over the years, and just as the staff at Costa discovered, these 'passing contacts' add up to something very significant. But the parable of the sower also reminds us that while many seeds may be sown, not all of them fall into the same soil. Some of the people who contact us may be drawn into deeper conversations, and are 'not far from the kingdom of God', while for others the contact is just a small moment in changing or confirming their experience (positively or negatively) of church. The next section identifies two particular groups of people that we meet – and warm contacts and wide contacts.

The people we meet

Warm contacts

The opportunities we have are still immense. In 2016 the Church of England conducted 43,000 weddings, baptized 112,000 children under 12 and helped 139,000 people through a church-led funeral service, whether in church or at a crematorium. At the heart of the major life event services are the core people with whom we have contact, who have come to us for help. Drawing on language from the retail and service industry world, these might be called 'warm contacts'.

Warm contacts are people who of their own free will ask for help, without having to be persuaded or coerced into an initial conversation. A while ago I was thinking that this year would be the year to get a new car, but I hadn't really done much about it until one Saturday I found myself with a bit of time on my hands and out of the corner of my eye saw the local Renault car dealer. I parked and went into the showroom. A salesperson approached and said, 'Can I help you?' I replied with the words every salesperson longs to hear: 'Yes, I am thinking of buying a new car.' And in that moment the salesperson knows that their task has begun, not just to get me to buy a Renault once, but potentially to become a lifetime customer of that brand (research around car sales indicates that there is a strong loyalty to a brand once purchased, with as many as 40 per cent of owners returning to purchase the exact same model next time for the leading brands: www.carscoops.com).

A warm contact is a person with whom you have a direct opportunity to converse, and who has made a choice to start a conversation with you. Each time the Church of England is in touch with those at the centre of a life event it is a warm contact opening up a chance for conversation, discussion, welcome, friendship and sharing the good news in a way that might lead to a life-changing encounter with Jesus. This illustration is not to suggest that we adopt a 'consumer model' for life events, but rather that we see the invitation to help as an opportunity to start a conversation. The figures and research show that people are still choosing to ask us to be involved in their special moment, and it is an immense privilege to be able to minister to them, showing God's love and grace.

Wide contacts

It would be very strange if a coffee chain didn't count its customers at a motorway service station on the basis that they were just passing by! Yet we can only 'guesstimate' the number of people who attend weddings, funerals or baptisms, as at present we don't collect statistics for attendance at life event services. Of course, I have stood in the vestry with my churchwarden after a Sunday afternoon baptism in church and asked her, 'How many do you think there were, then?' She usually replies something along the lines of 'about 80', and together we agree a figure to go in the register. But that figure is not collected as part of the gathering of statistics for mission. No one ever asks for the numbers we have encountered through weddings, funerals and baptisms. And when we don't count people, all too often they don't count. A cautious estimate of average attendance at each of these services as being around 50 means that we are potentially meeting around 15 million people each year through life events. This compares with the 2.6 million that are recorded as attending Christmas services of any kind (Church of England, *Statistics for Mission 2016*, Table 12, p. 28).

Those we meet as part of the congregation at one of the services marking a life event might be called 'wide contacts' – a broad group of people who encounter the hospitality of God's people as they share in an important occasion for their family and friends. Each of these statistics represents individuals, unique lives, surrounded by family and friends (or not, sometimes) who are unconditionally loved by God. Each moment – whether of loss or celebration – is a special moment for them on their journey. It is an occasion in their lives. In this sense it is completely different from the key times in the journey of the Church, when each year our special occasions, such as Easter, Pentecost, Christmas, become moments when we invite people to share with us. Instead, at these moments we are being invited to show God's hospitality as we meet people where they are, even if they are simply passing through for a moment.

Life Events

What we have discovered through all our research is that while we do not always, or indeed often, discover what positive impact the service may have had, we do begin to see that a negative experience makes it much more difficult to talk about faith later on. Negative experiences of church have a more significant impact than most other experiences. For example, if someone has a bad experience at the doctor's surgery, they do not leave saying that they will never go to any doctor again or will have nothing to do with the whole system of healthcare and well-being, and ensure that no one in their family ever does either. Instead, they moan, may choose a new practice, and get on with it. But we do know that after a bad experience of church people may decide never to engage with church or religion or God again. I recently met someone who had given up on church and faith after attending a church-led funeral for a family member. The whole thing had been experienced as cold and impersonal: 'He never mentioned her name once. Not once.' This gave a sense that the church really wasn't bothered about either the deceased or those who mourned. Sadly, in this case the person made a conscious and deliberate decision to look elsewhere not just for funerals but to meet her own spiritual needs.

There is no longer widespread cultural pressure that suggests that involving the Church at one of life's key moments is the respectable or acceptable thing to do, which means that those who do ask us to be involved are making a choice. The research that has been done explores why those who invite us make this choice. The research also considers how people understand staying in touch with church, and what might encourage them to become more involved over the years ahead. Those with whom we have the opportunity to have a conversation – the warm contacts – are at the heart of our ministry, but we also meet millions of others for whom there is the possibility of a positive, memorable experience of church. One vicar who conducts lots of weddings in a picturesque church says of the many young adults who come through the building, 'I don't know if this will be the first, the only time, they come into a church. So I need them to have the best possible experience I can give them.'

The positive experience or memory is a starting point, and each and every time a person has an opportunity to encounter church again that memory will be recalled, and, hopefully, each subsequent encounter builds on that moment. Through these encounters we pray that the Holy Spirit is at work, opening hearts and minds to the fullness of a relationship with God through Jesus. Part of the challenge of the work of the Life Events team is to discover what the local church might do that encourages people to build an active relationship with it and become active disciples. The next section explores the clues that have emerged about the thinking and actions which might enable us to create the opportunities for those we meet at Life Events to go further on their faith journey.

The big message – confidence, relationship, courage

It is now some years since we began to research and reflect on the insights we have gained around life events in the Church of England. We have shared detailed messages with thousands of clergy and lay people, and those insights are at the heart of this book, explored fully in the following parts of the book relating to baptisms, weddings and funerals. It has become clear that there are actually three simple things that lie at the heart of everything, three words that will begin to make a difference at a local parish level. After all the thousands of words that have been spoken, the hundreds of stories that have been shared, the three core words are: confidence, relationship and courage.

Confidence – be bold

The research clearly shows that we can have *confidence* that the people of England like what we do and actually don't mind us talking about God! We have discovered that those who have experienced a wedding, baptism or a funeral are positive about their experience. What we do, we generally do well, most of the time, and it is valued. There are insights that will help us to build bridges, improve welcome and encourage people on to the next step of their journey. There are also surprising insights into what it is that people appreciate and value about ministers, congregations, buildings and liturgy. The research did not show us that, to use marketing language, we have a bad product. But it did show us that we don't tell people much about it! We discovered that people don't mind us talking about the things of God, and that prayer is much more appreciated than we may have realized. The research helped us understand the extent to which people may have a tentative sense of prayer themselves, and how our offer of prayer for them and with them might be received. The research helps us all to be more confident in who we are and what we do, and above all to have renewed confidence in the gospel.

Relationship – make connections

In our research with clergy and lay ministers we discovered a great deal of anxiety about whether our services and our facilities were alienating people, and therefore a lot of expectation that fixing things like premises or service books would be the key to changing the way those we meet engage with us. However, a clear pattern emerged that showed that it is the way we build *relationship* that makes the biggest impact. Or to put it another way, it's the 'soft stuff', not the hardware, that matters. Having a warm building, comfortable seating and the highest-quality presentation will not draw people back, unless these aspects are accompanied by genuine smiles and interest. Over and again, the research revealed the central importance of welcome and hospitality, and this is something that is the ministry of the whole people of God.

This can seem quite challenging when many life event services take place either away from the church building, as with a funeral at the crematorium, or at times when few church people are present beyond the minister. Yet a pattern emerges that shows that when people meet people, when they discover the potential for friendship at church, this can be key in helping them want to find out more. In each of the life events particular aspects of relationship are important, including the way in which professional relationships can make a real difference around funeral ministry.

I recently had the opportunity to be a chaplain on a Thomson's cruise ship over Christmas, which was a wonderful experience. While on the ship I learned that Thomson's have one of the highest repeat booking rates among passengers. Working with them it soon became clear why guests want to return. It was not about the cabins, or the entertainment or the facilities, great as they are, but that the staff managed to create a real sense of community, getting to know people, building relationship, and genuinely serving people. Passengers return because they feel as if they are returning to people who genuinely want to see them again – relationship matters.

As I reflected on the experience, I realized that this reinforced all that we have discovered through our research – it is the genuine interest in wanting to build relationship that draws people back. The research insights and the resources we have developed will help us to do what we do as well as we can, but above all they help us to have confidence in liking the people we meet, and longing to draw them back. I am often reminded of the words of Adrian Plass, 'God's nice and he likes you,' and hope that this is what we reflect as we meet people who approach us for help at life's key moments for them.

Courage – take action

We thought carefully about the third key word before settling on *courage*. It became very clear across all the research that consistent follow-up is the real bridge from mission to discipleship. Meeting people at life events is an opportunity for the Church to reflect the love of God, and while for some it will be just a fleeting contact as they attend the special service to offer support to a friend or relative, for others there will be a real opportunity for someone from the church community to have a conversation. However, unless that contact is followed up with invitations and information, the chance of a person returning to church becomes much less likely. But it takes courage to keep in touch with people, especially if they don't even live locally.

One insight that emerged is the contemporary relevance of the issue St Paul identified in 1 Corinthians:

> *What, after all, is Apollos? And what is Paul? Only servants, through whom you came to believe – as the Lord has assigned to each his task. I planted the seed, Apollos watered it, but God has been making it grow. So neither the one who plants nor the one who waters is anything, but only God, who makes things grow. The one who plants and the one who waters have one purpose, and they will each be rewarded according to their own labour. For we are co-workers in God's service; you are God's field, God's building.* (1 Corinthians 3.5–9, NIV)

The courage to maintain contact with those we meet at life's key moments may mean accepting that the outcome may not be seen in the church where the particular event took place. But a pattern emerged that as long as the church was in touch, the likelihood of making future contact, albeit in a different place, perhaps even a different denomination, continued. The world of contact and communications has changed radically in the past decade, and there are more opportunities and means than ever to follow up afterwards with those we meet. Courage links back to confidence – the confidence that we have something that is worth sharing. People really don't mind hearing from us as we try to build on our relationship with them, a relationship that has echoes of the great relationship that God is making with us through Jesus.

Life Events

The opportunity to sow seeds is there when we meet people at special times in their lives. The following sections unpack in detail our findings about what makes for effective mission and ministry at each of the three big services: the baptism of a child, weddings and funerals. At the end of each section are suggested practical ideas and resources that can support parishes in this calling, which lies at the heart of the Church of England.

Part Two

The amazing journey: Ministry around the baptism of a child

Miriam nods. Jakob, next to her, smiles at him, sips his wine. 'You have a daughter now, Jim,' he says, 'nothing will ever be quite the same.'

'I know,' Jim says, and he smiles back at Jakob, overwhelmed with the newness of his baby daughter, with the sense of a life stretching before her like a blank page, waiting to be filled. (Laura Barnett, *The Versions of Us*, p. 133)

The birth or arrival of a child into a family is definitely one of life's 'big events'. Everything changes as routines are disrupted, emotions overflow and perspectives alter. Moods can swing from celebration to awe to anxiety in moments as the precious gift of new life is welcomed into the world. It is actually rare for the Church to be ministering directly at the time of birth – although there are lots of Christians working as midwives, obstetricians, doctors and health visitors, who may well be present offering professional support. There may even be a chaplain around to show pastoral care and explicitly offer prayer and praise to help put words to the wordless thoughts.

The Church becomes involved afterwards, when a family makes a decision to mark the physical start of life's journey by beginning a spiritual journey and asking for baptism. Each of the three life events that this book talks about is distinctive: marriage involves being part of a legal process as well as showing pastoral care; a funeral is primarily about pastoral and spiritual care; and baptism? The Church of England understands baptism as a sacrament 'marking the beginning of a journey with God which continues for the rest of our lives, the first step in response to God's love'. The Pastoral Introduction to Holy Baptism in *Common Worship* continues:

> *For all involved, particularly the candidates, but also parents, godparents and sponsors, it is a joyful moment when we rejoice in what God has done for us in Christ, making serious promises and declaring the faith. (Common Worship: Services and Prayers for the Church of England, p. 345)*

For the Church, baptism is more than simply celebrating and giving thanks for the arrival of a child. It is about new life, forgiveness, grace, overcoming darkness, and God's unconditional love. The work that has been done by the Life Events team is not about the principle of baptizing 'those unable to answer for themselves' – that is taken as a given in Anglican practice, as it has been for centuries. Rather, the research and thinking is about understanding what motivates parents to bring a child for baptism. How can we help them to make connections from their experience to the journey of faith and discover a lifetime of belonging and believing?

> *We come to the font, whether as a baby or an adult, empty handed, as we shall come to God at the end of our lives, offered a love which is a free and unconditional gift.*
>
> *Of course, each of us has to embrace the life we have received … I must eventually freely accept or refuse who I am as a baptized child of God. (Timothy Radcliffe, Taking the Plunge, p. 10)*

This witness to God's unconditional love and grace is beautifully expressed in a prayer used in some Methodist baptism services, at the moment just before a child is baptized:

> *For you Christ lived, for you Christ died, for you he rose again. For you Christ intercedes at the right hand of the Father. All this for you, before you could know anything of it. In your baptism, the scripture is fulfilled, we love because God first loved us.*

This part of the book comprises the following:

- Reflection on Scripture.
- Missional moments with families.
- Changing trends around birth rituals.
- Clergy concerns about language and liturgy.

- Six core insights from the research.
- Practical ideas about families, children, church and faith.

Biblical reflection: Jesus and the children

As part of the development of our thinking around baptism ministry, the Life Events team and our wider working group looked at various scriptural passages, beginning with our reflections on the parable of the sower, explored in Part One (p. 6). We then looked for more specific biblical references to baptism in the Gospels, only to realize again that Jesus himself does not baptize. Instead we were drawn to the story found in all three of the Synoptic Gospels, when Jesus welcomed the children and blessed them. In Luke's Gospel we read:

> *People were bringing even infants to him that he might touch them; and when the disciples saw it, they sternly ordered them not to do it. But Jesus called for them and said, 'Let the little children come to me, and do not stop them; for it is to such as these that the kingdom of God belongs. Truly I tell you, whoever does not receive the kingdom of God as a little child will never enter it.* (Luke 18.15–17)

There is something very contemporary about this story of people who want to access someone with authority or influence and those who have the power to give or refuse permission. We don't know quite why the disciples were so forbidding, but perhaps they had decided that they could control who was allowed to get close to Jesus. Perhaps they were protecting him, or perhaps they just felt that an important teacher shouldn't be bothered by what was almost certainly a group of women and toddlers. Jesus cuts right across all of this, and simply calls them into his presence, telling the adults to look at the children as exemplars of how we enter the kingdom of God.

As we looked at this story again we noticed three things:

- Welcome and inclusion – the children and families are encouraged to draw close and be with Jesus.
- The presence of Jesus transforms the situation – it is Jesus who intervenes, turning it from a day of difficulty, perhaps tension and conflict, into one of blessing and encouragement.

- We don't know what happened to them next – we have no idea, as with the vast majority of Jesus' miracles and interactions, what difference it made to their lives. We don't know if they were listening on other days, present at the cross, there in the upper room, part of the early Church – we just don't know!

I like to think that the story of the day they met Jesus was told and retold down the generations, and I want to trust that they were drawn onwards in their journey with God, but I don't actually know. We realized that we have to trust that God is at work, and this was important for us as we reflected on the impact of our own ministry around families we meet asking for baptism.

Baptisms: Missional moments

In 2016, there were 102,000 infant and child baptisms in the Church of England, and 65 per cent of those were of babies under a year old (Church of England, *Statistics for Mission 2015*, Table 14, p. 32). There has been a steady decline in the number of baptisms over the past decades, as society changes and it is no longer a societal norm or a mark of respectability to 'get the baby done' (although for some families there will still be a strong tradition). Those that do ask for baptism for their child are more likely to be making a positive choice rather than simply meeting expectations.

One of the biggest shifts is in the age of children being brought to baptism. As child health has improved and the risk of infant mortality becomes lower so the perceived need to baptize a child in the first few months has also changed. The split in recording the figures – those under a year old, and those aged between one and 12 – reflects a time when the vast majority of children baptized would be young babies.

I was recently looking at some family history records from the nineteenth and early twentieth centuries, which showed that every single child was baptized within six months of birth, the majority within the first few weeks. But things have changed and by 2015 a third of all baptisms were of children aged one to 12 years.

To get some insight into what this means, the parishes taking part in the pilot phase of this work were asked to count the number of baptized children aged between one and three and those aged four and over. We discovered that 70 per cent were in the age group one to three years old: the Church of England is baptizing a lot of toddlers rather than a lot of ten-year-olds! This is borne out by the experience of parish clergy, with many recalling that babies are now often around a year old when families arrange the service.

For each and every family this event is significant, and it is also an important moment in the life of the Church. Every week the Church of England welcomes an average of around 2,000 children under 12 through baptism, and each baptism gives the local church an opportunity to have direct conversation with around six people. There will usually, though not always, be two parents involved, a child and a minimum of three godparents. These are the 'warm contacts' discussed in Part One (see p. 12) – people who of their own free will have asked for help and support at one of life's big moments. We get a chance to talk to them, engage with them, encourage and welcome them, sharing God's hospitality and love and the good news of Jesus. For many of the clergy we spoke to in the focus groups this is at the heart of why this ministry matters:

'It's a privilege to mediate God's love to the new baby and family.' (Vicar, Blackburn diocese)

'When people come in through the doors and want to find out about baptisms, we think, as a church, great – because a baptism is a beginning with Christ. That's what it's about, the building blocks of faith and it's about simple steps, about people finding out how they grow in God.' (Vicar, Birmingham diocese)

The numbers of warm contacts the Church of England has through baptism ministry could average around 12,600 people per week. The vast majority of those will be in the age group 18–45, as these are the primary years for building family life. In addition to these warm contacts, baptisms can attract some of the largest congregations of the week, and the numbers of guests coming to such events are almost certainly increasing. Many churches talk about how the numbers are so large that the service has to be held at a separate time in order to fit everyone in the building. It is not uncommon to hear of 100 or more guests at a baptism service, but assuming an average of 70 guests at each one, these 'wide contacts' may amount to around 154,000 people each week – a staggering 7.6 million people each year. This compares well with recorded attendance at Christmas services in 2016, or the further five million attending civic or school services during Advent. Many of those in these groups will be the same people:

that wide group for whom the Church of England is 'church' at pivotal moments in their life.

Each of those 150,000 people is on a journey – and as those leading services, we don't know how near or how far they may be from God. We also don't know the details of the story each of them is carrying with them – whether the day is one of celebration and shared joy or one that has shadows of pain overlaying it. The research conducted for 'Talking Jesus' (Barna Group, 2015) suggested that while very few people indicate that going to a wedding, funeral or baptism directly brought them to faith, almost one in five suggested that 'life events' were important factors on their journey. There is also the possibility that those attending a family christening have been at more than one such service in a relatively short space of time, as the following fictionalized story of 'Kate', based on many conversations, illustrates.

Missional moments: The story of 'Kate'

'Kate', aged 29, comes home from work one day to find a large hand-written envelope on the mat – always a cause of excitement these days! She opens it to find an invitation to the christening of the first child of one of her friends from university. Kate went to the University of Warwick, and this particular friend stayed in that area after graduation. So on a lovely weekend in early June Kate finds herself in a village church in Warwickshire for a lovely service with old friends. Not long after that, she finds herself in a church in a different part of the county for the wedding of another old university friend – another lovely service and a great weekend away. That's only one of three weddings she goes to that year – the others are held in a hotel and a castle. Then in September Kate is chatting over coffee with a friend from work who has just come back from maternity leave, and this friend invites her to be godmother to the new baby at the christening which will be in November. Kate, christened herself as a baby, is thrilled – this is a first for her, and she takes it very seriously, thinking hard about her role and what it means. So when November comes round she finds herself in a church not far from where she works for a very special service.

Then at Christmas she heads back to her family home, some 150 miles away. When she gets there her mum tells her all the local news, and includes the fact that there is a new vicar – and she's heard some good things. So she suggests that she and Kate go to church, as they did when Kate was a child, and they find themselves at a midnight service. Just a few months later Kate's grand-dad dies suddenly. He has lived all his life in the same village, not far from her parents, and although not a churchgoer, there is only one place his funeral can happen – the village church. So Kate finds herself in yet another church – she has attended five different churches in 12 months.

However, it is not until another two years go by and a new colleague at work invites her to a social event that Kate is drawn in to the life of a local church, where her discipleship finally springs to life and she becomes part of a local congregation.

It is very difficult to track this kind of story, to know the journey that people have been on as they discover faith. Some things encourage and some things hinder, but being welcomed at one of life's key moments, standing alongside friends as they mark the event, may well be part of an overall positive experience that helps. In the commercial world, leading companies understand that creating good memories is a key part of building long-term loyalty, recognizing that experience and memory affect future choices (KPMG, 'Making Memories').

Rituals around birth: Changing times

Patterns in how birth is marked and celebrated have changed over the last few decades, and while none of these changes actually affects baptism directly they may have implications for how those around us respond. Two of these changes are of particular interest: the growth in 'baby showers' and secular naming ceremonies.

Baby showers

One big change in the last five years has been the growth in 'baby showers'. A major indicator of the popularity of these parties is the amount of space devoted to baby shower partyware in card shops. Just three years ago there was very little, but now most stores have a dedicated section of materials available, from balloons to tableware to gifts.

Baby showers originated in the USA, and are a party given for the mother-to-be usually around the eighth month of pregnancy, often coinciding with the beginning of maternity leave. Traditionally, they are organized by the expectant mum's female relatives and girlfriends, and attended only by women. They are usually very sedate affairs, often arranged around afternoon tea (after all, this is late pregnancy!) and involve the giving of gifts to bless both mum and the expected arrival. Sometimes dads and other male family and friends are included as well.

A baby shower has nothing directly to do with baptism of the baby, but the fact that an event has happened with family and friends late in pregnancy may well lessen the need to gather family together to celebrate. A baby shower may not replace a baptism, but it may mean that baptism is more likely to happen later on, perhaps after the arrival of further children, suggesting that the family is complete.

Some churches are beginning to recognize the importance of support and contact with families during pregnancy. For example, one church holds 'beading parties' for those in late pregnancy. The women of the church gather with the mum-to-be and each chooses a bead to be made into a special bracelet which the woman is encouraged to wear during labour, reminding her of the prayer and support that is offered.

Naming ceremonies

The second trend is the growth of 'naming ceremonies'. At present these are very small in number, and generally to be found in more metropolitan or 'alternative' areas. The research undertaken as part of the background to the work around baptism suggested that only about 3 per cent of families had held such a ceremony. The ceremony can be held anywhere, may be led by a celebrant, and focuses on the child's name as the core of the event. For some the naming ceremony will represent a definite choice to mark the occasion without reference to a particular religious viewpoint:

> 'We know we want to do something to celebrate our baby's arrival, but we're not religious so a christening wouldn't feel right.' We hear this a lot and this is exactly *where humanist naming ceremonies come in.* (www.humanism.org.uk: Ceremonies/Naming)

There may well be a significant cost in organizing a naming ceremony – from around £190 upwards. Our research showed that while there was some interest in the idea of promises to protect and bring up a child well and a place for formally introducing the child to the world, there was also a sense that it had insufficient gravitas and required quite a lot of effort to put together.

'Feels like a watered-down version of Christening. Like Christmas, now totally commercial, with no religious meaning.'

There is a church service that may meet the needs of parents looking for a different approach, acknowledging that sense of wonder and gratitude for the arrival of a child: the Service of Thanksgiving for the Gift of a Child, known colloquially as a thanksgiving, 'blessing' or sometimes 'dedication'. Some parents want to give thanks but are unsure about a faith commitment, and this service does not preclude baptism later on. However, our research found little public awareness of the service, and it is not widely used in the Church, with only around 5,000 services recorded each year. Families were puzzled by it, often thinking it was 'American', as the only usage of the word 'thanksgiving' with which they were familiar was in the context of Thanksgiving Day. Some parents began with positive comments as they looked at the text of the service, until they realized that it didn't have any symbols to give a deeper significance. For others, especially if the vicar and church bring creativity and meaning to the service, thanksgiving will be a positive choice to make.

Baptism: Clergy concerns

The possibilities for meeting children and families through baptism ministry is both exciting and challenging. The focus groups we held with around 300 clergy helped to identify some of the issues that face parishes as they minister to families at one of life's most significant moments. There were worries about whether it is best to hold baptisms during regular Sunday services or at a separate service, with different reasons to support each option. Some clergy were very positive about welcoming families in Sunday worship, while others felt that the chance to focus on the family exclusively worked better at a separate service.

However, one of the biggest concerns from clergy was the question of whether families would ever be seen again. During the baptism service the words 'in baptism the Lord is adding to our number' are said confidently and yet I know that in the midst of a chaotic service with parents and godparents and guests apparently struggling to engage, those words can feel more like hope than substance. But the reality is that in baptism God is at work, and this was made very real for me when I spoke at an event in Coventry diocese, which happens to be my familial home.

The Bishop of Coventry introduced me by highlighting my connections with his diocese, including the fact that I was baptized at St John's, Hillmorton, confirmed at St Leonard's, Ryton-on-Dunsmore, I even picked up the leaflet that led to ordination on a visit to Coventry Cathedral. During the first coffee break a woman came up and introduced herself to me with the words: 'I was also baptized at St John's, Hillmorton.' After a bit of conversation we worked out that we grew up 20 doors apart on the same street and were in the same reception class at infant school, but my family moved away when I was six years old. We both came from aspirational working-class families where 'getting the baby done' was routine. She was baptized in September while I was baptized in December that particular year.

Truth to tell, you could have met me ten years later and nothing much would have changed, and even 30 years later my spiritual journey was on its roller-coaster route. But here we both stood – 50 plus years later, both ordained priests in the Church of England. Then she told me of another girl, from a similar background, also baptized that quarter at the same church, who is now a minister in the United Reformed Church. Three girls, three baptisms – and I found myself wondering, just who had prayed for us at that time? In those days there was something called a 'Cradle Roll' and I suspect that people faithfully prayed for the babies who were baptized, whether they knew them or not. God was at work, and the Lord was adding to our number – just not for a few years, and not in St John's church! One of the biggest difficulties for us in our ministry with families through baptism is that very often the timescale and geography that God works through is not the same as ours and we will not see the work come to fruition. Paul echoes this problem in 1 Corinthians 3.6:

> *I planted the seed, Apollos watered it, but God has been making it grow.*

Meeting families through baptism: Six core insights

It is against this background that the research unfolded, listening to those who come for baptism and those who have decided against, exploring the issue as to what is really making these 100,000 families make this choice. At the heart of all the thinking has been the core question as to what makes families come and then what makes them stay, and from that we have developed a particular approach that will help and support parishes. Confidence in what we do, the building of relationships and the courage to follow up are at the heart of the findings across all our research.

Six core insights emerged as central from the research, which was specifically around the baptism of a child under 12:

1 Understanding language makes sense.
2 Parents have serious motivations.
3 Godparents really matter.
4 Building relationships is central.
5 Symbols and words are significant.
6 Follow-up makes all the difference.

Each of these insights has helped to identify key opportunities that are important on the journey that families make together with God's people. Each insight will be explored next, together with practical suggestions and resources that will help local parishes in their ministry.

1 Understanding language makes sense

Right at the beginning of this work, I went out on to the High Street to look for various products to build a prayer station that would reflect some of the themes that emerged from the research and those things that are the heart of baptism. I found cards, balloons, gift bags and presents with the word 'christening' prominently displayed. However, it was more challenging to find a card or gift that featured the word 'baptism', other than in a Christian book store.

This widespread use (outside church circles) of the word 'christening' was fully reflected in the research. We discovered that regardless of location or back-ground, most families call this service a christening, with the word over ten times more likely to be used as a search term. Within specialist social networking sites such as Mumsnet, the difference was even more marked.

An Omnibus survey (a population-wide survey to find out opinions, attitudes and behaviours) completed as part of the research revealed that for 57 per cent of people the preferred term was also 'christening', rising to 68 per cent of 35–44-year-olds. It became very clear that to the public this service is called a christening.

This meant that the team had to do some very tough thinking and prayerful reflection. We talked with liturgists and church historians and went back to look at our research again. Then we made the bold decision that for all our public-facing materials we would use the word 'christening' but that almost the first sentence would be, 'During the christening your baby will be baptized.' This small sentence represents the first step in introducing enquirers to new language and new concepts. It may also help to draw parallels with the difference between a wedding and a marriage, as during the wedding service a couple are married. When a mum rings up to ask if she can 'book a christening' she is simply using the language that she knows. As the first step back towards a faith of which she may only have faint recollections yet still thinks important enough to summon up her courage and ask for help, this tentative question is all she has. 'Booking' is the word that people use for everything else they organize and 'christening' is the ordinary, everyday word. Sarah Lawrence, a PhD student, has done some linguistic work around the use of the words 'christening' and 'baptism'. Her findings are very interesting, as she discovered that for 'ordinary' people the word 'baptism' was seen as part of the language of an elite group, including clergy.

> *Christians have good reasons to have some wonderful associations in their minds with the word 'baptism' … [but] by using 'christening' we are not communicating a lack of seriousness about religion, but rather a joyousness and celebration.* (Sarah Lawrence, 'The history of the words "baptism" and "christening"', available at churchsupporthub/baptism/articles)

Although there was some initial resistance and concern among clergy about the use of the word 'christening', experience has shown that the shift in language is helpful in meeting people at the place where they begin. In Acts, St Paul met with the people of Athens and began his conversation by talking about the things they already recognized and knew, referencing the 'unknown God' before going forward and leading them towards the God who wants to reveal Godself to people in Jesus. By using the ordinary language of 'christening', churches discovered they could also begin to help people further onwards in their journey, as these clergy discovered during the year-long pilot phase.

'When I stopped worrying about the words they were using, I found I could have real conversations.' (Vicar, Rochester diocese)

'The language of "in a christening service your child will be baptized" ... was a wonderful way of resolving that dilemma and helping us to bounce the language around.' (Vicar, Leicester diocese)

'This sense of journeying has been helpful for me to use, because it's something that we do together, rather than "this is what you are coming to and we're going to do this to you".' (Vicar, Coventry diocese)

Out of the research and reflection a whole fresh visual and verbal approach was developed, using journeying imagery, drawing on both the motivations and thinking of parents and the liturgical language already available in the Church. The introduction to *Common Worship: Christian Initiation* talks of the interaction between journey, story and the 'Way' as images for the Christian life, and in helping an individual to find their place within the story of faith as experienced in both the local church and through the Scriptures.

Journey is a major image in the narrative of Scripture from the call of Abraham through to the itinerant ministry of Jesus and beyond. As an image of human life and of the passage of faith it allows both for the integration of faith and human experience and also for the necessity of change and development. (Common Worship: Christian Initiation, p. 9)

The emphasis on journey through words and visual images is helping families to understand that baptism is the beginning of something for their child rather than an end in itself. After a year of using the materials that have been developed, and making small adjustments in language and approach, 95 per cent of the parishes who took part in the pilot phase reported that they felt families were developing an understanding of baptism as a beginning.

The language that families use to talk about faith or about their own experience of spirituality may be very different from that used inside the Church, something that echoes through the research. This is evident not only in the use of the words 'christening' and 'baptism' but also in the language used to talk about spiritual things, serious feelings and the experiences of church and faith. Listening carefully to the language and experiences of parenting helps both to bring understanding of parents' motivations and to build bridges to church and faith, and the next section explores these insights.

2 Parents have serious motivations

In a culture where it is no longer obligatory or a significant aspirational marker, there are still thousands of families who want to have their child baptized in the Church of England. For some of those families faith will be an intrinsic part of their lives, expressed through active churchgoing and daily discipleship. But many others are either historic, fringe or even non-church attenders and yet they still want this ceremony for their child.

It is the motivation of the latter group of people that the research wanted to understand, so interviews were held with over 1,000 families defined as irregular churchgoers (those who attended fewer than six times a year, including Christmas). Some of these had positive attitudes towards church, while others were fairly negative in their expectations and engagement.

Choosing to have a child baptized arises out of a complexity of motives, feelings and ideas, and most respondents selected several of the choices offered. However, the reasons that emerged can be summarized into three main areas, around:

- Past experience.
- Right choices.
- Community.

Each of these themes are unpacked below, drawing on the thinking and experiences of the parents who took part in the research.

Past experience, future expectation

First, families are already on some kind of faith journey themselves, or at least have had some kind of positive experience of a church-based activity in their lives. This might mean that they have positive memories of a church-led activity, such as Sunday school or youth group or even a church school, and this is something that they want their own child to experience. It may be that they look at other family members and see that church and faith have been positive factors in their lives, and again want to see a foundation laid for their own child. At least 64 per cent of research respondents had some kind of connection or experience of church when growing up; at least half have either parents or grandparents who currently attend church at least sometimes.

I was talking to some parents about the forthcoming christening for their child, and because I was immersed in the research findings I found myself asking questions differently. I asked the dad in particular what it was that made him want to have the little one christened. He started to talk about his time as a Cub Scout, and in particular about the impact that large services in the cathedral had on him. He spoke of being awed and inspired by going into the biggest space he had ever experienced, and a sense of something more, and then said, 'and I want my little one to touch that too'. Of course, we know that you don't need to be baptized to join Scouts or attend an amazing service in a cathedral – the important factor is that the parents have a positive memory of a faith experience in their own childhood.

This has a number of implications for the Church of England. It reinforces the importance of the work we do with children, whether through schools, clubs or other activities. It also means that as we meet with parents, there is an opportunity to explore their memories and discover what has already been going on over the years. One of the most useful responses to a parent's story or reason is, 'Tell me why that is important to you' – it opens up conversations and sometimes allows a deeper level of insight to emerge.

For some there is also a sense that the journey of faith, and of life, is started in the presence of God:

'It's the first step of giving them a choice on faith and saying, you have been baptized into this faith, God knows you're out there and if you want him he's there. If you don't, that's fine … I feel like they have been blessed and someone is looking after them because they have been introduced to God.'

Life Events

Parents have a strong sense that baptism will give their child choices in later life – it is a starting point for a journey, which may or may not lead them to a lifetime of faith. Seventy-nine per cent of those interviewed said that giving their child the choice of a Christian future influenced their decision to have a child christened. At first glance this can seem at odds with the Church's understanding of baptism, which involves a decision to turn to Christ, and might be understood as 'nailing your colours to the mast' rather than opening up choices.

Martha, from Hertfordshire, talked about her understanding:

'In the future my children will have a choice of whether they want to carry on being Christians or not. You know, I believe Christianity is not something that is compulsory. It is a personal choice, and therefore, it will be up to them, in future, whether they want to carry on being Christians or not.'

As Martha puts it, 'Christianity is not compulsory' – all of us make choices during our lives whether to walk closely with Jesus or at times even to walk away altogether. Many committed Christians are aware that their own children and grandchildren, godchildren, nieces and nephews are presently choosing not to follow, in spite of their baptismal promises. But we never stop praying for them, trusting that one day they will choose to turn again and follow.

Respondents spoke of the foundational nature of baptism, and for some a related anxiety is that without this foundation the opportunity for an awareness of faith, religion and spirituality may be lacking:

'I feel it's important for my children to know as much as possible to make a choice later in life. Yes, the Christening is a very important part of this as it sets the steps for my children to explore later in their life: it's an important start to their religion. Children don't learn enough in schools these days about faith and religion.'

For some parents there is also a sense that having their child baptized rekindles their own spiritual awareness and response. When we talk about this research at events, there is nearly always someone present who tells the story of how the baptism of their child brought them back to their own relationship with God through Jesus, sometimes even setting them off on the path that led to ordination.

Leanne and Darren Bell were ordained in Newcastle diocese. They talk of how until they had their youngest child baptized eight years previously they had rarely been to church, but the warmth of welcome and their own feelings renewed their faith journey.

'*I remember feeling very emotional, it felt like I had been away somewhere unfamiliar and I had come back home.*' (Leanne Bell, Church of England Facebook, 29 June 2017)

Research respondents expressed this more tentatively, with a renewed awareness of prayer and of their own need to know more so they can answer a child's questions.

'*My faith has got stronger, I think. I certainly didn't pray before I had my daughter, or prayed not an awful lot. Maybe if someone was ill or something like that then I might pray, but now every night I do, because I've got my daughter … I just started doing it, and that was it. So every night I pray.*'

One small change churches can make in response to baptism parents is to encourage and affirm their life of prayer, and listen to the journey of faith that the parents may be on and be wanting to open up to their child in the years ahead.

Right choices

Closely related to the idea of wanting a child baptized as part of a faith journey is that of baptism being a way of giving a child a good start in life. In some ways, it is easy to dismiss this as some kind of aspirational ideal, akin to opening a savings account or laying down the best wine, yet listening more deeply to the language and motivation is very revealing.

Wide research with parents shows that the arrival of a child is one of the most intense and transformative experiences of their lives, and it often catches people unawares in its emotional impact. Parents will feel a deep sense of awe and wonder, together with a heightened awareness of their own responsibility and limitations. Some of the dads in the research talked of 'an incredibly weird feeling you won't feel about anything else'. The quotation that opened this part reflected the immense emotional impact that hits with the birth of a baby. You can watch this lived out on the Channel 4 reality programme *One Born Every Minute*. The premise of the programme is simple: each episode follows three or four women and their partners as the mothers give birth. Often the programme has a theme, such as older mothers, absent fathers, or parents with lots of children. Another theme is younger parents, where the mum and dad are in their late teens. Very often the person labouring with the young woman is her mother, while the young father stands awkwardly to one side, as if to say, 'What's this got to do with me?' But then (after an appropriate amount of drama and noise) the child is born and fairly quickly handed to the uneasy-looking young man. Almost without fail, he will begin to weep, overcome by the enormity and wonder of the moment.

In those first few moments every parent, mum or dad, simply wants the best for their child, even if the odds are stacked against them. Parents long for their child to have a better life, a good life, to make the right choices and decisions as they go forward, and they are often acutely aware of how difficult this might be.

'You hope that the world isn't really changing for the worse, but I fear that it is, so you worry about the world you're bringing the child into … the wider issues, which you have no control over.'

New parents often have a heightened awareness of the possibility of danger of the world, and of their abilities to equip their child to negotiate all that lies ahead. At one stage in the research, members of the team made a visit to the National Baby Show at the NEC, to consider whether the Church of England might have a stand there in the future (which we did: but that's another story!). As we walked among the numerous stands offering 'transportation systems', nappies, bottles, toys and clothing, we suddenly came across one for the RSPB. Yes, the Royal Society for the Protection of Birds, which, apart from a fleeting thought about storks, seemed a bit out of place at a baby show. But a conversation with RSPB staff there revealed some very similar insights: a sense that parents want their child to have a wonderful, idealized childhood and a corresponding fear that all they value is under threat and may not be there in the future for their child to enjoy. For the RSPB, and probably other charities too, this means that family membership is a great opportunity for parents both to enjoy the benefits of outdoor interests and to contribute to ensuring that the good things they value last into their child's future.

When parents begin to talk about baptism as giving their child a good start in life, it is often expressed in language about ethics and values, the building blocks that will enable their child to negotiate all the choices that lie ahead.

'I like the ethics and the things that the Church believes in and the way that they encourage you to bring up your children.'

'The values and principles of the Church are the basis of law in this country, so even if he decides not to follow any faith the basic teachings are essential.'

Early childhood can be a time when parents are aware of all that is harmful in the world – which means that talking about evil in a wide sense and sin in a personal sense becomes very relevant. Most of us are acutely aware of the mistakes we have made in our own lives, and want our children to make good choices. Learning centres for children, whether church, community or academy, now build a great deal of their ethos around values, which may well be rooted in faith traditions. Schools will talk about kindness, generosity, honesty, courage, peace and other similar values, helping children to learn how to live these out in their daily lives. When parents begin a conversation about the christening with clergy or baptism visitors it may well be a good opportunity to explore what they mean by values and ethics – which ones matter to them, how they envisage building them into their lives, and what happens when family life fails to live up to expectations. It may be that for families who are on the edge of church, the starting point for understanding what Christianity is about may be more 'Good Samaritan' than 'Prodigal Son'. Parents may find it easier to talk about what it means to be a good neighbour before thinking about what happens when we fail to live up to the standard that we set for ourselves, let alone the example Jesus has given us. The conversations, contact and time spent with parents is where we can begin to introduce them to Jesus, who not only shows us the way to live but makes it possible.

Community matters

Alongside the sense of journey and the desire to help a child have a good foundation for life, the most important reasons parents give for wanting a child baptized at a christening are often to do with people – with celebration, community and belonging – although less than half (41 per cent) suggest that the opportunity for a celebration was a major influence. For many families, this will be a very special time to gather and be with friends and relatives from near and far. For those parents who are not married, it may well be the first opportunity they have had to meet together and be 'family' – although there is no sense from the research that a christening is a substitute for a wedding. It is a distinctive, joyful occasion, and may well be one of the milestones on the way towards marriage.

Contemporary relationships often move through stages of co-habiting, shared purchases, shared home ownership and children, before getting to a wedding, which is the crown of their relationship. This was borne out by the research done with couples for the Weddings Project, which showed that marriage is still an aspiration and ideal for many (see Gillian Oliver, *The Church Weddings Handbook*, p. 12).

One of the hallmarks of the christening for families will be the party – and the word 'christening' will be used to describe the whole day, as in this quote from Martha:

'Both of my christenings for my children, were lovely. But, it involved the family, celebration and community. Marcus' christening: we did it at home and we enjoyed the family surroundings. Later on, when we had Marvin's christening, we had to hire somewhere because the family was getting bigger and bigger. It was such a huge celebration for us.'

At first glance, Martha's comments are confusing: it sounds as if her son was baptized at home rather than in a church, but as she continues it becomes clear that she is talking about the party, the gathering of people to be with them on the day, which was hugely important.

Gathering with friends and family at life's big moments is a part of how we live out community and belonging. The 'wedding breakfast', usually known as the reception, follows the marriage ceremony, but I have never yet heard a colleague say, 'They are only getting married so they can have the reception.' Likewise, a gathering of friends and family will usually follow a funeral as memories are shared and support offered – and again, no minister would ever say that someone is only having a funeral so they can organize a wake! Yet as clergy we do sometimes say that families only want a baptism so they can have a party. There is nothing intrinsically wrong with a party – Jesus seemed to go along to social gatherings quite frequently, and the great biblical image of a gathering of the nations at a banquet sounds like a wonderful party, especially with wine and oil that flows abundantly. It is right and good that people should want to celebrate together and the arrival of a child is a particularly joyful event.

The sense of belonging to a community is also an important reason for baptism. Liturgically and theologically, we talk of welcoming a child into the family of God's people where they will always have a place. For Martha, not only was the physical gathering of friends important, but also the sense that her children now had a place to belong:

> 'It will mean a community that is welcoming to all. Their doors are ever welcome to anyone who wants to walk through. You know. Christianity has no boundaries.'

Community is very important to young families. Research around contemporary relationships suggests that young mothers in particular can become very isolated. They may live in affordable housing in the heart of a new development with few community gathering points, perhaps far from parents and support networks. Until just a few weeks before the birth, new parents may be part of a work and social hub, but as the initial shock and excitement at welcoming the little one home fades, and one partner is left alone, community can seem a distant dream. A BBC documentary shown in January 2016, *The Age of Loneliness*, explored loneliness at different life stages. The director, Sue Bourne, was motivated to make the film after reading that young people were as lonely as older people. In 2015, a survey by Netmums and AXA found that more than a quarter of the new mums interviewed admitted to feeling lonely. Both spending time with family and finding a community to belong to were viewed as important.

An interesting indicator of the importance of community that emerged from the research is the location of the church where the baptism takes place in relation to where the family live. Many respondents talked about being allowed to have the christening in a particular place that was linked with family history or personal circumstances, the implication being that it was not their 'parish' church. One way to understand this desire is to think about community in two ways – horizontal and vertical. Horizontal community is those people we know in our various social circles at any given time – work colleagues, social contacts, immediate family. Vertical community is community that stretches back in time – our grandparents, for example, and other connections. This has become increasingly important in our culture, as evidenced by the growth of interest in genealogy websites and TV programmes such as *Who Do You Think You Are?* When a couple ring up a church 15 miles away and ask to have a christening there, the reason may well be to do with a 'vertical' link such as family history. What seemed particularly significant in the research is that the relationship between the place of baptism and that of future churchgoing is not straightforward. Those who were or became actively involved in church after the baptism were more likely to be going to a different church from the one where the christening happened. Being welcomed and given permission to be in that place is really important.

> *'Having our daughter christened in the church we did has made us feel closer to the church; my husband and his sister and nephews were christened at the same church and our nephew is head choir boy.'*

> *'Both my children's christenings were very traditional. They were both per-formed in the same church I was baptized in and my mum also got married there'.*

The decision to baptize a child who lives in any specific parish is a legal one: canon law requires that we must baptize a child who lives in the parish, allow-ing due time for preparation. However, the decision to baptize a child who lives outside the parish is primarily pastoral, as canon law requires only that we seek the goodwill of the incumbent of the parish where they reside. Many, if not most, families have little understanding of parish boundaries and church rules and may hear a well-meaning encouragement to explore their local church as a refusal. The Church of England is a national church, and a family may see involvement in a church that is different from where the baptism happened as ongoing relationship and community.

3 Godparents really matter

The third 'core insight' that emerged from the research was that there was one group of people who were significantly more important than we had realized. The top reason, by a short head, given for wanting a child baptized is so that the child can have godparents, with 91 per cent saying that this was an influence on their decision (87 per cent identified blessing as most important, and 89 per cent making a good start).

Further questioning showed that the godparent role is very important to families, with 83 per cent of respondents agreeing that the relationship should be taken seriously. One reason for this may be that having godparents had been important in the lives of the parents. Around two-thirds of respondents had some connection with a godparent, or were one themselves, and this proportion was even higher in those with few church connections. Godparents are valued as people who will build a long-term stable relationship with the child, playing an active part in the child's life as a role model and offering nurture and guidance. Sometimes parents tend to project forwards into the teenage and young adult years, when a voice offering advice from outside the family might be appreciated. Someone who could act as confidante and counsellor at a time when parents may find it less easy to do so is especially valued. Great importance is placed on morality and ethics, sometimes above spiritual or religious guidance, which resonates with the idea that parents believe that in baptism children are being given a good start in life or being helped to make good choices.

> 'It was like that with our godparents: they aren't overly religious but I know they will help, support and guide my daughter on the right moral path. Which in my opinion is more important than whether they are religious themselves.'

> 'It's very important that they are involved in her life, to teach her the right ways and when she gets older decides to follow God. Then hopefully they would help her decide that and guide her in the right way.'

Choosing godparents can be a difficult decision, with many parents honouring long-standing friendships and looking for those who are willing and able to make a long-term commitment, rather than choosing short-term contacts.

Many adults will talk about how important godparents have been in their life. At a wedding I went to not long ago, for example, it was clear that the bride's godmother had been a key support over the years and a highly significant figure. And at a special birthday dinner for an 85-year-old, one of the 14 guests present was her 60-year-old goddaughter, a relationship that had been lifelong and life-enhancing for both of them.

Many people in our regular congregations will be godparents themselves or have godparents. It is a special, valued relationship. However, the Church gives little or no guidance or encouragement as to the choice of godparents, beyond explaining that godparents must have been baptized themselves. This can become a major issue if parents have already chosen godparents before contacting the church, and may well not have realized this requirement.

> *'The church tells parents the importance of godparents, but they don't support the godparents themselves. The church didn't meet up with them beforehand or even require it … in our case they gave the godparents a certificate and wanted them to be baptized, that's the only involvement they had. One of ours has never been a godparent before so doesn't really truly understand their role, but I chose her because of her good values and trustworthiness … I know that if anything was to happen to us they would always be there to help, guide, support and love our daughter.'*

Sometimes there is confusion about whether godparents are automatically legal guardians – as a question on a recent BBC Radio 2 phone-in revealed. Churches may need to explain the difference, but perhaps also explore the idea that being there for their godchild if anything happens may be more about shared memories and values rather than a specific legal role.

The importance of godparents was one of the most significant findings to emerge from the research, and has led to some very specific initiatives and responses, including the establishment of an annual Godparents' Sunday. This was celebrated for the first time in 2016 and is already growing in significance.

It takes place on the Sunday immediately before the first May Bank Holiday – based on the idea that the long weekend, for most people, might make travelling for visits easier. This means it will always fall between 30 April and 6 May. A range of special resources has been developed and churches are encouraged to pray for godparents, invite them to visit, bless them and generally support the relationship (see www.churchprinthub.org). These include pin badges to give away with the words 'Praying Godparent' and 'Blessed Godchild', words carefully chosen to help affirm that godparents have a spiritual relationship alongside the social and emotional connection.

One vicar who took part in Godparents' Sunday in 2016 was amazed at how many godparents and godchildren came to a special Sunday service, and having re-established the relationship he ended by talking about confirmation to the adults. Another church was able to start a new family service after re-establishing contact with families and godparents who lived in the parish at a Godparents' Sunday celebration. Much renewed contact was made using social media, with prayers offered and memories shared. Some churches now give information about Godparents' Sunday when a family arrange the baptism, implying straight away that godparents are important to the church as well as to the family.

Parents have a web of reasons for choosing to have a child baptized at a christening, some of which are easily articulated, while others are more deeply felt. They may not be expressed in obvious spiritual or faith language, and yet the desire for community, wanting the best for a child, seeking God's blessing and opening up the possibility of a faith journey are also echoed within the church's story. Meeting parents is an opportunity to build a relationship with God's people and the way in which that relationship starts and develops can also echo the way in which their relationship with God through Jesus might unfold over the years ahead. It is this opportunity that is explored next.

4 Building relationships is central

From the moment when parents start to think about celebrating their new arrival with family and friends, through contacting a church, making arrangements for baptism, getting ready for the day, and the day itself, the church has many opportunities to meet and talk with parents and others. These moments are central in the experience people have of the local church and open up the possibility of a long-term relationship being built. The research gave us insights into the impact that such meetings can make and helped us develop resources and practical ideas to support parishes – but research is only about patterns that emerged, not predictions as to what will happen. However, this section is at the heart of the work we have done around welcoming families into church through the gateway of baptism.

Do parents know what's possible?

While in some areas there may still be a steady stream of families approaching church to enquire about a baptism, there are also opportunities to raise awareness with local parents about the possibilities of beginning a lifelong journey of faith. Bearing in mind the deep feelings around the arrival of a child into a family, church can be a place that offers practical ongoing support as well as a space to mark those feelings with a special service. For some parents that will be a christening, for others it may be a 'thanksgiving'; for many more it may simply be involvement with a church-run toddler or baby group.

But many will be afraid to even ask an initial question, so finding ways to encourage contact will be appropriate, such as putting up posters. There may be opportunities to use the 'Start an amazing journey' leaflet (available from www.churchprinthub.org). This leaflet invites parents to consider enquiring about an initial conversation, and is ideal for distributing to nurseries, mother and baby groups, mums and bumps groups, and for displaying in church. It may also be useful at local community events, whether church-run or not, for the local church to have some kind of stall to raise awareness of all that they do. If a parish has a large number of young families, an article about christening or godparents in a local newspaper or magazine or community blog could be helpful in developing understanding and raising awareness. An attractive poster is available that can be displayed in church or community groups encouraging parents to find out more, together with a special leaflet with information about Thanksgiving services. (These and other resources can be found at church supporthub.org or www.churchprinthub.org.)

The importance of welcome

Whether families approach church because they already know that they want a christening, or whether they come as the result of information made available locally, the first response they receive is vitally important in establishing the relationship that lies ahead. It may be a bit of an apocryphal story, but it seems that there are those who greet the enquiry, 'Can I book a christening?' with the response, 'Sorry, we only do baptisms here.' Regardless of what might happen in the future, it is really good for the response to any query to be warm and congratulatory. After all, they don't have to call and it has probably taken a lot of courage to make that contact. The research showed that for over 25 per cent, contacting the church or meeting the vicar for the first time causes people to feel anxious or uncomfortable, so putting them at ease as soon as possible is important. Whether it is the vicar, an administrator or baptism visitor who answers the initial enquiry, answering with a smile in your voice can make a real impact, together with a response that opens up the possibility of conversation rather than closing it down.

'Let's meet and talk about what might be possible' begins a relationship, whereas a straight 'No' closes it down. We discovered during the pilot phase of the research that holding the first meeting around the time of a church service can be really helpful, giving parents the opportunity to come into the building and see that people actually get involved! For example, arranging to meet over after-church coffee can be a good first step for families, but it is important that there is an overall attitude of welcome when strangers turn up.

There will be more than one place in this book where the importance of welcome is mentioned. I have yet to meet the church that describes itself as unfriendly or unwelcoming. Yet I know from experience, and that of countless others, that being a visitor at church can be intimidating, isolating and exclusive. I remember being at a very lively suburban Anglican church service where the minister invited people to gather in twos and threes to pray. I felt such an outsider as people pushed by me to gather with those they knew – and if I as a church-confident stranger felt that way, how much more difficult for the total newcomer. Recently I found myself in McDonald's for the first time in years, feeling out of place and uncomfortable, saying inane things like, 'I used to come here years ago.' Everyone else seemed to know what to do whereas I wasn't even dressed in the right way (dog collar and business wear) and was confused by the menu. It was being smiled at by a kind family in front of me in the queue that helped to make the whole thing less intimidating. It made me reflect again on how strange it must feel for those entering church after many years, with only a faint memory, or perhaps no memory at all, of what happens there. (For more on this, see 'Stepping into the unknown', churchsupporthub. org/baptisms/articles.)

Apart from Sunday worship there may well be other opportunities for families to make contact with church before or as they begin to talk about christenings. Even if they haven't been to any church activities, an awareness that a church cares about and encourages young families makes a big impression. The research showed that knowing that young families go to the church and that the church gives an impression of caring is an important factor for over half of our respondents. However, it is worth noting that around a third of families had no idea what the church had to offer to them.

The ministry of welcome is a ministry of the whole people of God, and when parents (or wedding couples or the recently bereaved) appear in our churches, a kind smile and a warm hello will help to lay the ground for building a relationship. Ultimately, families begin to connect with church when they have a sense that this is a place they can belong, and the first impression that this is even a possibility happens in the initial moments of contact, however that takes place – through a website, printed materials, a phone call or face to face. A recent review of the UK businesses with the highest ratings for customer service and customer loyalty showed that warmth and personal touch permeated every point of contact, and above all, first impressions are hugely important:

> 'The first thing that happens shapes our view of what happens next – the process of priming. If the initial experience is outstanding it is like placing a large deposit in an emotional bank account. If what happens next is positive, it benefits from confirmation bias; alternatively, if what happens next is negative, the customer will be more forgiving. However, if the initial experience is poor, the reverse is true.' (KPMG, 'Making Memories')

The primary question in the forefront of parents' minds is getting the date fixed – when they make contact with the church it may be that they already have a firm date in mind, particularly if they have little understanding of how church life functions. As knowledge of church diminishes in our culture, it is increasingly likely that parents will not realize the particular challenges facing churches when trying to finalize dates. We often feel embarrassed or silly in a situation we are unfamiliar with, or when we ask a question that reveals our ignorance. Sometimes that means we become defensive, or very apologetic – and parents trying to book a christening are no different. But if we want to open the possibility of an ongoing relationship, then both the tone and the content of our reply will matter.

Once the date is agreed, it is worth collecting contact information for both parents and godparents so that you can be in touch with them with dates and times for toddler groups, church services and any preparation programme or visit that you are going to make. Many churches are finding the Pastoral Services Diary (www.pastoralservicesdiary.org) an invaluable tool for managing contact details and being reminded of the key moments you need to make contact as you build relationship with the family. You can read more about this in Part Five.

Parents are likely to be looking for information in a number of different places as they get ready to have their child baptized at a christening. The research showed that as well as speaking to families and friends, particularly those who had recently had a christening, parents turn to websites and social media for information. It is helpful if the church offers simple information at the time when the baptism is agreed – and this might include directing them to the Church of England's christening website (www.churchofenglandchristenings. org), which has a wealth of information about the service and about each of the roles associated with the baptism. A simple leaflet is also available which has the key points parents need to know, and most importantly will list the contact details for the local church, so that parents know how to get in touch in the weeks or months between the time of booking and the day itself.

Getting ready for the day

One of the best opportunities to build a relationship with a family will come through meeting them at a baptism preparation course or visit, and nine out of ten respondents had been offered some opportunity to prepare for the event. However, only around a quarter felt that it had been insisted upon, with the majority feeling they had a choice about whether to spend time with the church before the day.

The nature of baptism preparation also varies enormously:

- 80 per cent had a chat with the vicar.
- 31 per cent had a chat with someone else from the church.
- 23 per cent had a few sessions, like a short course.
- 22 per cent went to church a few times.

There is clearly some overlap in these figures, with some families likely to do more than one of these options. But it is perhaps worth noticing that the most common type of preparation is perceived as a 'chat with someone'. However, the research showed an interesting pattern in that those who had a short course or went to church a couple of times were more likely to have a closer relationship with the church after the baptism. Attending a short course or being encouraged to go to church are the situations where relationship-building is cemented. Families may well have an opportunity to meet other parents who are at a similar stage of life to them, and new friendships can be formed. For example, at one church parents are invited to an evening session (with wine!), where they are able to meet the vicar and people from the regular congregation, and also begin to form the kind of contacts that mean they are building relationships and connecting to a community. This pattern is something that parents may be familiar with through organizations such as the National Childbirth Trust (NCT), where long-lasting friendships can be forged through shared experiences.

At first glance one of the most reassuring messages from the research is that baptism preparation is doing a good job, with the vast majority of respondents feeling well prepared. Almost two-thirds agreed strongly that they understood both the significance of the event and the responsibilities they were taking on. However, less than half felt that they were made aware of any expectation of a future relationship with church, while those who were involved with church afterwards were the most likely to have realized that there was more than just a one-day event involved. However, this sense that baptism preparation is being done well seemed to be at odds with the perception of clergy in the focus groups, where one significant underlying concern was around baptism preparation and whether parents understood what they were doing. The research with families suggested that while the church is doing a good job at preparing families for the service, it may be doing less well in suggesting that baptism is the beginning of a lifetime journey of faith.

'Prior to the christening we were reasonably well briefed about the event. Our local vicar made us feel at ease about the process and talked us through any question or queries we had. I can't say that we fully discussed the religious significance of the baptism.'

'A couple of weeks prior to my son's christening we met with the vicar after the usual Sunday service to go through the christening and what would happen on the day.'

For most families, the mechanics and logistics of the day are bound to be at the forefront of their minds. They want everything to run smoothly and their anxieties are likely to be about such things as where to sit, when to stand, when to speak, as these are what they are unfamiliar with. It is true for most of us when we take part in a public event or ceremony: I can remember various graduation days where the most pressing concerns were about timings, negotiating stairs, how long to shake hands for, rather than any deep and meaningful thoughts about what the event meant for the rest of my life!

One practical solution may be to make a clear separation between rehearsal for the service and an exploration of what baptism is about. I don't think I have ever met a clergy person who thinks that the wedding rehearsal is the right time to do marriage preparation, or would expect that to be the moment when couples start thinking about what this will mean for their life ahead. Most of us use the rehearsal to do just that: walk through the choreography and script of the service, checking that everyone feels confident enough to relax, enjoy and engage with the ceremony fully.

> *'Before we got married, we had marriage preparation and I think my husband went to a sort of get ready for christening meeting, which I wish I would have gone to because men don't really relay things very well. I don't think you get the same kind of support in preparing a christening as you do with getting married. And yes, you do go through the nuts and bolts of it. But I'm not sure there's more about why you're doing it and the reasons. It doesn't have the same seriousness as a wedding.'*

Whatever baptism preparation programme your church offers, it is worth thinking about having a rehearsal, about how the families will meet others from church, and perhaps also about where to hold the preparation programme. When we present the research findings at one-day conferences, we always show a short clip from an episode of *Pramface*, a BBC 3 comedy ('The Edge of Hell', first shown on 8 January 2013). In this episode, the young parents (who are not 'together') are preparing to have their as yet unnamed daughter christened. Although the context is Roman Catholic, the scene where the parents arrive at church for a pre-baptism talk is excruciatingly familiar – and funny.

The dark and shadowy scene opens with the young parents, Laura and Jamie, struggling into the church down some steps with a pushchair. Laura looks round with trepidation. As clergy and regular churchgoers we may be so comfortable with the building that we easily forget how anxious and uneasy people can feel about being in church. The first words most of us ever heard in a church were probably along the lines of, 'Ssh, be quiet', which can leave us with a lifelong sense that this is a place where there is acceptable right behaviour that some people know and others don't. So although it is really good to get families along to church to see where the baptism will happen, we also have to work hard to make them at ease.

Meeting the vicar

It is equally true that the idea of a visit from the vicar to the family home fills some people with trepidation. A clergy colleague who went to visit a family at home discovered that they had bought special cups and saucers for the occasion, nice biscuits, 'posh' tea, and kept apologizing for the state of their home. One thing I have noticed over years of baptism visits is that it is not uncommon to arrive and find that 'daddy' has mysteriously had to pop out on some urgent errand. Then, with incredible timing (which always makes me think that he was lurking in the shed or street), he reappears just as the visit is coming to an end! Research for the Weddings Project clearly identified a 'white coat effect' for people when meeting a vicar – the concept that our blood pressure is raised just because we are at the doctor's surgery. But meeting in the vicar's study can be a far from easy option for fringe church people. One of the oddest things about clergy (or so removal companies always tell us) is that we own large quantities of books, visibly displayed on groaning bookshelves. I remember children from one particular parish looking at them with awe in my study and saying, 'Are these yours?' Then, when I answered in the affirmative, they replied: 'But what are they for?' The study can seem a very intimidating place to some people. Depending on the particular parish, arranging baptism preparation in the church hall or even a local café may feel more accessible to young parents, especially if they need to bring the pushchair with them. But wherever you arrange to meet to talk through all that the christening will involve and mean for them, encouraging people to come along to church is an invaluable part of their experience.

As well as thinking about where to hold the baptism preparation meeting, it is worth listening carefully for any expectations and perceptions people have that may turn out to be unfounded. The humour in the video clip from *Pram-*

face mentioned above is largely built around the mismatch of understanding between the lead couple, Laura and Jamie, Father Thomas, and the other couple attending baptism preparation, Richard and Amy. Much of this is about the notion of original sin and the nature of hell:

FATHER THOMAS   Err … so, so, as I say, it's, it's really more about becoming part of that community.

RICHARD   And to make sure they don't go to hell if they die.

JAMIE   She's not gonna die!

AMY   No, goodness, no!
Everyone relaxes.
But if she did and she wasn't baptized, she will go to hell.

FATHER THOMAS   Well, let's not get ahead of ourselves here, Amy.

JAMIE   I thought it was limbo anyway.

RICHARD   *(cheerfully)* Limbo is hell. It's a part of hell.

FATHER THOMAS   Looks doubtful.

RICHARD   Isn't it?

FATHER THOMAS   Well, it's the er … edge of hell. I think there's a theological debate to be had here, but now's maybe not the time. Or the place.

RICHARD   She'll probably still be able to hear the screams of the wicked from there though, wouldn't you say?

FATHER THOMAS   Again, let's not get too hung up on the screaming.

JAMIE   *(to Laura, reassuring)* She's not going to hell.

RICHARD   I'm just saying, logically, they'd be making a lot of noise. What with the burning and the suffering.

FATHER THOMAS   OK, the … ermm … nature of the afterlife is a great mystery but – I believe – God is merciful.

JAMIE   Yes. Yeah.
Laura sighs with relief.
Nobody's going to hell.

AMY   As long as they're baptized.
(*Pramface*, Series 2, Episode 1)

The important thing to note here is that this programme will largely have been watched by 16 to 30-year-olds and may well reinforce confused and half-formed ideas about what the church believes, or what baptism might be about. And those watching may well not be equipped to distinguish the nuances of different theologies and practices across different denominations. When parents and godparents are invited along to baptism preparation they may come with all kinds of ideas, worrying that there will be questions that they have to give the right answers to or some kind of test they need to pass before the service can go ahead.

There are many courses available for baptism preparation, and some churches develop their own material. As well as thinking through the content of the course, it is worth taking time to make families feel relaxed and reassured about the process. Newer courses include *We Welcome You* by Jacqui Hyde (CHP, 2016), which offers tried and tested interactive ideas for talking with families over one or more sessions. This course is grounded in much of the thinking that emerged from the research with baptismal families, and is flexible enough to work over a short course or a single session. An alternative approach, ideal for working with a cohort of new parents, is *Starting Rite* (CHP, 2015), developed by Jenny Paddison, a vicar in Leicester. This wonderful short programme focuses on meeting people during the year that mothers often have as maternity leave, and introduces parents to core spiritual concepts as a forerunner to the decision to have a child baptized.

Affirming godparents

Earlier it was noted that godparents are hugely important people, and it is definitely worth reflecting the significance of their relationship to the families during baptism preparation. Invite them to come along and take part, or it may be possible to use Skype or something similar to include godparents in the pre-baptism visit or course. Whether or not the godparents are present, taking time to discover why parents have chosen the people they have, to explore the history of the friendship, and celebrate the commitment that is involved, helps to show that the Church takes godparents seriously. A good thing to do at this stage of building a relationship is to offer a special thank you card. This was developed and designed as a direct result of the research, and is given to the parents by the church, and the parents give it to the godparents, thus cementing a three-way relationship. (This is distinct and different from a certificate, which might be given at the service.) The card (available from www.churchprinthub.org) is very simple and reminds godparents of four key things that they will do during the years ahead, including prayer and introducing the child to faith:

- Being there – how we spend time, listening, playing, enjoying, encouraging.
- Part of the family – over the years, sharing special times.
- Good choices – advice, wisdom, insight, help.
- Sharing faith – prayer, church, blessing, values, confirmation.

The most valued thing the card does is give a reminder and encouragement to pray. Included with it is the gift of a fridge magnet, which states, 'Loving God, bless my godchild today', so inviting godparents to pray for their godchild, other children in their family, and perhaps children in the world, each time they see the magnet.

It is impossible to overstate the warmth of response to this simple idea. At the National Baby Show we also offered a prayer fridge magnet to parents saying, 'Loving God, bless my child today', and gave both magnets away to parents passing the stand. Each day you could count on one hand those who declined: the gift of prayer is valued. Confidence in who we are and in the good news we have to share is one of the very simple discoveries at the heart of all the research we have done, and prayer is one of the greatest resources we have to offer and something we can affirm in the faith journey of those we meet. It may not be about offering a lot of formal prayers, but giving simple, practical, physical prompts that encourage those tentative initial forays into prayer that are part of the first steps of the lifelong relationship with God through Jesus that is there to be explored.

On the day

The day of the child's baptism is a very special day for a family, and there will be a lot to think about and prepare. Families will be planning the celebration, worrying about what to wear, concerned that all the guests make it to the right place at the right time, synchronizing decorating a venue with food deliveries and so on. In the midst of all this, they need to arrive at the church ready for the event that will stand at the heart of the day and mark the beginning of a new life. It can be very helpful to see the parallels with a wedding day.

It is also a very special day for the Church – getting ready to welcome a new person into the body of Christ of which we are all part. We have to make sure candles are ready, the font is filled, certificates are written and that we have enough service sheets for everybody to join in – or at least attempt to join in, or look as if they are. For both families and the church much preparation is needed, whether the baptism is part of a 9.30 a.m. regular service or at a special time just for the baptism on a Sunday afternoon.

Does the time of the baptism matter?

One thing we discovered through the research is just when baptisms are taking place. Canon B21 requires that baptism takes place during public worship, unless there are good pastoral reasons for doing otherwise. The Church of England's annual statistics for mission on infant and child baptisms do not identify when baptisms take place, so the information that emerged from the large quantitative survey is a good indicator of the likely pattern that exists. Overall, 38 per cent of baptisms took place within a main act of worship, with the remaining 62 per cent being held in separate services. People tended to be happy with whichever type of service they had. Those who had the baptism as part of an ordinary service often made the point about being welcomed into a community, whereas those who had the service separately valued the sense of it being personal and focused. They appreciated the fact that children and guests did not have to sit through a lengthy, unfamiliar church service. But they also found the service to be rather minimal, with little feeling of being welcomed into the church, and the contact was likely to be only with the vicar.

'We felt it was nice for the baptism to be part of the service as it welcomed us and our son to the congregation.'

'It was nice that it was part of the morning service because then it was like my son was welcomed into the church and everyone saw him. It was part of the everyday life of the church as it should be.'

One significant pattern that emerged in the research was that those who have their child baptized in a main service are more likely to become church attendees in the future. There are all sorts of reasons for this, but it connects with some of the other findings indicating the importance of meeting other people, and feeling a sense of welcome and belonging, things that are difficult to experience if the only contact with church is the Sunday afternoon baptism service itself. It reinforces the importance of giving families an opportunity to experience church beyond the baptism service.

Lots of churches find it difficult to hold baptisms in the main worship service – perhaps the church is literally not big enough, or there may be so many baptisms that it is overwhelming for the regular congregation. If those present at a separate service are warm and engaging, then meeting the vicar and one or two others will give an impression of a friendly church, likely to be welcoming in the future.

In some cases, churches encourage families who have had a separate service to return to a regular Sunday service to be welcomed, perhaps to receive a candle or a certificate.

'They invite you to come back for the first family service following the christening, at which you are supposed to be welcomed into the church so all the children that have been christened with their parents are invited to the front of the church and there's a proper welcome from the Vicar. These are the children that have been christened. And they talk about them and everybody claps and that's really lovely.'

Increasing the amount of contact that baptism families have with church is one small change that made a big difference to the ongoing relationship in the pilot parishes. For some churches, this meant an increased confidence in suggesting that the baptism takes place in Sunday worship, whereas for others it meant finding ways of helping new families to meet regular worshippers. For example, the initial meeting might take place over Sunday coffee, rather than in an office or at a 'vestry hour'; or a stronger link might be made with lay people who are present at the baptism itself.

Involving the whole people of God

One of the challenges facing churches can be the attitude of the regular worshipping congregation towards baptism families. One vicar who took part in the pilot phase of the research talked of how when certain members of the congregation bumped into her in the street they would say something like, 'Is it a baptism on

Sunday morning?' If she replied in the affirmative, the response then would be, 'Oh well, I will see you the week after, then.' Many churches notice that if Sunday worship includes a baptism at least some of the 'regulars' will be absent. Yet the ministry of baptism is a ministry of the whole people of God.

A key strategy in changing attitudes to welcome turned out to be inviting regular members of the congregation to pray specifically for individual baptism families. Once people commit to praying for someone a relationship begins – that's why sometimes I feel God prompts me to pray for people I find difficult. When we start praying, we are required to think about those people as individuals rather than just a problem. Several of the pilot parishes began to involve the regular congregation in prayer around the ministry of baptism – and changes began to happen. People began to make gifts for the babies and children, and there are some wonderful stories of creative expressions of welcome, including cakes being made, angels being knitted. In one church, a patchwork shawl is made with squares contributed from lots of the regular worshippers, then a label is added to indicate that it is a gift from the church and in the service the child is wrapped in the shawl as a sign of being embraced by the community. The vicar above went on to talk of how, a short while into using this new strategy, she met a member of her congregation in the post office who asked for the date when baby Jane was being baptized – so that she could make sure that the gift she was working on would be finished in time.

Prayer is one of the ways the regular congregation can support baptism families, and the making of small gifts may be a part of showing welcome and hospitality. Giving those with little previous contact with church a chance to meet people is also important; even if a family meets only two or three people as part of baptism preparation or at the church on the day, it can make a big difference. But perhaps one of the best ways of involving the whole people of God is through welcome at an ordinary Sunday service, whether the baptism takes place in a Sunday service or separately. This resonates with the findings from the 'Talking Jesus' research (Barna Group, 2015), which asked people to identify factors that influenced their journey to active Christian faith: apart from being part of a Christian family, the next most important event was simply going to a church service. Looking for opportunities to bring those who approach us into contact with who we are, not just in the words of a formal service but in the midst of a welcoming community, might turn out to be a surprising part of discovering the fullness of God's love revealed in Jesus Christ.

The quality of the relationship we offer has a great impact on families who come to us for the baptism of a child. That relationship can be fostered from the first moment of contact with smiles and warmth, and that same relationship will underpin what actually happens in the service. It is the service itself that is explored in the next section.

5 Symbols and words are significant

At the heart of the clergy focus groups was a deep concern with the words of the liturgy. This was explicitly named as something that made it difficult to engage with those attending a baptism service. It is also implicitly part of concerns around understanding and fears about parents feeling hypocritical or confused. The research with parents revealed a very different experience of the service, with many positive recollections of the day as parents talked about what was special or significant for them: memories that stayed with them for a long time afterwards.

The word 'significant' is important, as after a service parents may well be unable to recall specific words or phrases yet will look back on deep and important memories about what happened that day and all it meant to them. The relationship between word and experience in worship is at the heart of this apparent disparity between the worries of clergy and the experiences of families.

The liturgy of the Church of England is often understood by ministers as being about the words that are used, and a great deal of emphasis may be placed on the intellectual content of what is going on. Yet many of us know that our relationship with God is hallmarked by experiences that come to us in a variety of different, multi-sensory and emotive moments, which may be hard to articulate in words, at least initially.

My own mother was not a reader. To her, a book meant a copy of the magazine *Woman's Own*. So when as a pretentious teenager I announced that we were going to watch the BBC's showing of Shakespeare's play *Romeo and Juliet* she was less than impressed. But this was the olden days, so there was only one TV in our house and as I said that I had to watch it (for educational reasons) she hid behind her magazine while I adopted the pose of the interested student. As the play unfolded my mum slowly began to engage, and by the end she was weeping with the best of us as the bodies lay across the screen. But if I had asked her to identify the pivotal line in the script marking the shift towards tragedy, she wouldn't have known. It was the experience that had engaged her emotions rather than the intellectual analysis and comprehension of the text.

There is a BBC Radio 4 series entitled *Soul Music*, where a song that is known for its emotional impact is examined, and in parallel the story of someone for whom it was personally significant is presented, together with some technical analysis. 'Bring Him Home', a deeply emotional song from the musical *Les Miserables*, featured in series 22, episode 1. A woman who knew nothing of the technical skill behind the song talked movingly about how it had become part of her relationship with her daughter, threading through the ups and downs of life, becoming part of her life and death story. Then composers, lyricists and performers shared their insights, and my own appreciation of the power and meaning of this song deepened appreciably; but the song remains potent even without the technical insights. In our spiritual explorations, impact often comes before the questioning that leads to a deeper level of knowledge, and perhaps a deeper relationship with meaning.

In his recent book *Something More*, John Pritchard writes about journeys of faith and talks of how for some there is a sense of an unfolding journey, whereas for others there is perhaps a moment, a revelation, where everything makes sense. He writes of 'letting go and being surprised', describing various testimonies and encounters with faith, drawing on all kinds of experiential images:

> *The spiritual journey can start by letting go at last of the arguments and resistances that have kept this dimension of life in a box with a warning that the contents may seriously damage your health. Equally, it may start with the unpredictable eruption into our lives of some experience of the spiritual/divine that we didn't seek but can't deny.* (p. 126)

It should not be a surprise then to discover that when families bring a child to baptism the service is significant not because of any intellectual grappling with words but because of the meaning found in the overall experience. The candle and water are consistently named in the research as the most personal, memorable and significant moments of the service, followed by any prayer or blessing that uses the child's name (blessing is the term parents will probably use to describe the signing with the cross). Alongside this was a sense that they were truly welcomed, a tone usually attributed to the vicar:

'The vicar was a lovely lady … she made other parents feel comfortable in church.'

This reflects one of the few things that parents were worried or embarrassed about in the service, although fewer than half of respondents mentioned any concerns at all. The top three worries about the service were singing out loud, standing at the front and the behaviour of children. Only 7 per cent expressed anxiety about saying the baptism promises – the same number as were worried about simply walking into church – and only 4 per cent had any concerns about understanding the words of the service. This resonates with the findings about understanding explored earlier, which revealed a high level of understanding of both responsibility and significance among parents.

Personal and special

One very important aspect of the service for parents is that it should be personal and special. However, the good news for the church is that around baptism this simply means the things that we do anyway – it is not about fancy tricks or elaborate stage manoeuvres, but instead the giving of a candle, using the child's name and offering some choices, where appropriate, about hymns and readings.

'I didn't want to sort of change everything for us. It was about us joining them, rather than making it fit us. I thought they made a really nice effort anyway, so I felt that everything they did, that man doing that nice speech, and to pick our hymns, I thought that was really nice.'

'I really liked that my daughter was given a candle; this was given to one of the children in our family to hold during the service. We were given cards for the godparents and one for our daughter.'

Above all, families talked about the need for the service to be traditional, with less than 10 per cent expressing a view that the service should be anything other than this.

'Traditional is more meaningful. Nowadays everything seems too dumbed down or made to be in synch [in] a way that it doesn't offend anyone.'

'Traditional' is another of those words that may have a different resonance for those outside the Church compared to those of us within it. Previous research for the Weddings Project found that 'traditional' tended to convey the meaning that something had importance that goes beyond the everyday. Parents (and couples) use it when they are describing something that has stood the test of time, something of value beyond their own experiences. In church circles, 'traditional' may have acquired an almost pejorative meaning, assuming that something is old-fashioned, irrelevant, perhaps even lifeless. A different way of understanding it might be the phrase 'hallowed by use' – there is a clear sense that the words, practices, symbols and space all hold layers of meaning that have stood the test of time.

> *'Our service was traditional, but informal and relaxed. Too many people regard church as stuffy and uncomfortable.'*

The words 'special and significant, traditional, yet informal and relaxed' seem to sum up the way in which the baptism service is experienced at its best. The challenge seems to be less about the words of the service and more about how we build and reflect relationship, relaxing so that we can do the things that surprise and entice people further. A major insight into this came at an event in the funeral world. (This story is also shared in the funeral section of this book, but it is worth including here.)

I was at the Ideal Death Show, in plain clothes, at a seminar about public speaking given by a leading teacher on this mysterious art. Her basic premise was that we need to use two modes – 'cat mode' and 'dog mode'. Neither is right or wrong – each is appropriate at different times. 'Dog mode' is when we are warm and engaging, reaching out towards people with energy and enthusiasm – think Labrador or Golden Retriever! 'Cat mode' is when we occupy a more formal, distant space, only inviting people to join us when we are ready. The speaker ended her description of 'cat mode' as formal, distant, cautious and reserved, followed by the words, 'like vicars'. Public perception is often that clergy and church indeed always operate in 'cat mode' – so when we do things that move out of that into the warmth of 'dog mode' it takes people by surprise.

One of my favourite quotes from our research interviews is:

> *'The vicar makes a difference, their character … such a good atmosphere yet still doing their job.'*

You can almost hear the incredulity in the respondent's voice as their preconceptions and expectations were overturned; somehow the vicar balanced both 'cat mode' and 'dog mode', combining traditional, serious and significant with relaxed and friendly. The baptism liturgy is full of moments of warmth and friendship, but also has moments that are profoundly serious and significant. The most important of these occurs when the family and guests are invited to gather around the font (another strange church word: every English adult knows that 'gather' means standing 10 feet away – except the children!). Even in the most lively and challenging of gatherings the actions around and with the water are the moments that have the most seriousness and will be memorable and special. One mum found herself remembering the christening as she held her baby after his bath:

> *'I thought of the vicar holding my baby that day, and then I remembered God's love holding my baby.'*

The baptism liturgy is rich in symbol and drama, with moments that take the things of everyday life and transform them into experiences of God's love and grace. The words we use are an integral part of how meaning is communicated, and it may well take a lifetime of thinking and reflection to unpack the full significance of all that is spoken and promised in the service. The research with families suggests that the impact is as much in what we do and how we speak as the words we use – our concern needs to be equally for the 'soft stuff' as for the 'hardware' of liturgical texts.

This research was conducted before the alternative texts were authorized, but there is no doubt from clergy responses that for many these texts feel easier to use. Those leading the service may find they are more able to focus on the things that help to build the longer-term relationship, and enable people not only to remember the symbols but also to engage with the words that are said.

In practice: Loving the liturgy

Although there are many choices available that can help to make each baptism service special and distinctive to the church where it takes place, there are really only three types of baptism service:

- Baptism within a Sunday Eucharist.
- Baptism within a Service of the Word (probably a 'Family Service').
- A separate baptism service.

Regardless of which kind of service is chosen, there is a basic shape to the liturgy, a framework to which the minister and others contribute to help make sure that it is a real opportunity for an encounter with God. One of the most important mind-shifts is to think of every baptism (or thanksgiving) service as an all-age or multi-generational service. Of course, every worship service is an all-age service, with people present at different stages of life and experience. But many churches offer a service with a particular emphasis on age diversity, calling it something like all-age worship or family praise, with special care being taken to choose specific hymns, prayers and readings. But all too often we put in hours of preparation only to find that the age spread is somewhat smaller than we expected, with one small baby and lots of grandparents.

Whenever and wherever a baptism service takes place, every generation will be represented: babies and toddlers, a scattering of school-age children, young adults, grandparents and increasingly great-grandparents. The principles and practices of good all-age inclusive worship are the same as those that can help to ensure that worship is more accessible to those unfamiliar with church, with a focus on relevance and simplicity, but without becoming patronizing or childish or losing any of the seriousness of the event.

> 'I do like the fact that it does still feel like a ceremony rather than a party or something.'

This resonates with the sense that the service needs to be 'traditional', bearing a weight of meaning and significance for both the church and the child at the heart. Baptism is a serious matter, and yet there are good ways in which this seriousness can be made warm, accessible and engaging for all who are present, whether familiar or unfamiliar with church. There are five basic 'sections' to the service – gathering, listening to the story, the baptism, responding, going out – and ways to help families, guests and the regular congregation participate in each moment. These are each explored below.

Gathering

The tone of welcome and inclusion is set right from the beginning of the service as a worshipping community forms for that time and place, though it can be difficult sometimes even to get the baptism party to come into the church so that the welcome can begin. People think that once they are inside the church they may have to behave differently, to sit still, and be unable to talk. I visited a church recently where a Sunday morning baptism was taking place and one of the nicest touches was that the door was kept open so that latecomers could enter easily, and a team of lovely people were on duty to welcome, help with information and make guests feel at ease. I was with a child whose particular needs meant that it was important to be able to move in and out of the space quickly and often, and the open door and warm smiles made it easier than it might have been. Those coming to the baptism, whether in a regular or a separate service, are coming as invited guests of the child's family, yet are entering into a space that may not be familiar to either host or guest.

The language of 'guest' is both inclusive and egalitarian in the context of a church service, and may be worth reflecting on as we welcome those invited as guests by the parents of the child. The 'baptism party' – parents and god-parents, sometimes augmented by siblings, grandparents and others – may also be helped by particular attention and welcome. Reserving seats is useful, but it may not be helpful for them to be in the front row, especially for those unfamiliar with church, as it is not possible to respond to other people's actions, like knowing when to stand or sit. One church developed a practice of making sure that Sunday regulars were spread about the church, and equipped to be encouraging and helpful to baptism families. There is sometimes a debate about using service sheets, especially in churches where there are screens. Although we are communicating to a generation used to screens, people's residual memory of church will include holding something and a service sheet is also a good guide to the overall shape of an unfamiliar event. Perhaps you could personalize the service sheet with details of those who are to be baptized, or include them in a notice sheet, even with a photograph.

Photographs can themselves be a thorny issue. Today's young adults have a very different attitude to photography from that held by those of us who grew up in the age where a Polaroid camera was amazing! My parents had one or two very formal wedding photos; my own generation had the special album, full of more stylized photos, but now taking photographs is not a special activity but more akin to a way of responding to the world, almost the language that is spoken.

The Revd Kate Bottley has a disarming way of speaking to guests at a christening. She reminds them that the child is too young to remember the day and will need their help in the years ahead to recall all that happened. Then she invites, even encourages, everyone to take as many photos as they like. I have seen the effect this has: it disarms and charms people. They no longer feel that they have to 'get one over the church' by sneaking a picture, and once the pressure is off, people relax and the taking of photographs may even lessen. The growth of social media in recent years means that it may be more appropriate now to ask people to refrain from posting pictures until later in the day, rather than limiting the photography itself.

Telling the story

Once the appropriate words of gathering have been used, including words of informal welcome, a full Sunday service may move on to include penitence, the Gloria and a collect, before the central activity of telling the story begins. Even in a separate service a short portion of Scripture will be read, often the account of Jesus' baptism or perhaps the occasion when Jesus welcomed and blessed children, and if the baptism is in a regular Sunday service the readings for the day should be used. There are so many good translations and story versions of the Bible available that it should be possible to read from something that is definitely Scripture, but in contemporary language. A friend attended a baptism in an all-age communion service where after the Gospel reading was read from the Bible, it was presented by the local 'Open the book' team, much to the delight of the local schoolchildren, who recognized those taking part from school assemblies.

Then there will follow a sermon or talk – and it is in this space that the links between the world of Scripture and the Church, the baptism that is to take place, and the lives of those present can be made. Good baptism talks will often use the symbols of the service itself or the symbol of the journey to make connections, and there is much rich imagery from Scripture and contemporary culture that can be drawn on to engage those present. One such story comes from the 2012 London Olympics. The swimmer Chad le Clos won a gold medal, and as his father made his exit he was grabbed by Clare Balding for a quick interview. It was one of those 'So, Mr le Clos, how do you feel about your son?' interviews. Mr le Clos simply said; 'That's my boy. My beautiful, beautiful boy.' And everyone had to reach for the tissues.

There was something so sincere and profound in those few words. Retelling the story at a baptism service, I simply add something along the lines of: 'That was what God was saying to Jesus that day [the day of his baptism], and it's what he is saying right now to your child and to each of you here.' The story connects the 2,000-year-old gospel with the common experiences of parental love, helping families discover the fresh relevance of the good news into their lives.

Promises and baptism

Once the story has been told in a way that is relevant and engaging, the service moves to the heart of the event as the baptism itself takes place. Much drama, movement and symbolism is involved, and whichever words are used enable people to engage with the power of symbols that speak in tandem with the words. Although respondents in our research did not mention finding the words of the service problematic, the question was explored further because they are so important. In one focus group, families who had decided not to have a child baptized found some of the words from the service troubling. In particular, the notion that they have to repent of sins and talk of death and redemption was disturbing.

'It's the wrong terminology. "Repenting sins" is not appropriate as they've just been born.'

'It's meant to be such a nice day and they're so negative.'

Although the language of sin may be unfamiliar, parents may be deeply aware of the potential for harm in the world and of the mistakes they have made in their own lives. Talking through the promises during baptism preparation in a way that makes sense of their hopes and fears, regrets and disappointments, may help to bring greater understanding of these words. It is also worth noting that people generally find it easier to talk about God than about Jesus, and as other research such as 'Talking Jesus' has shown, there is a lot of confusion and lack of knowledge about the significance of Jesus as a historic figure, and all that he means for the Church. Yet perhaps that too resonates with the idea of a faith journey. Over and again, Jesus and his followers simply invited people to come and see, to find out about Jesus, get to know him and discover his words and sayings.

Among those who choose to have a child christened there will be a wide range of different understandings about what it means to be a Christian, with a strong sense that it is about ethics and values rather than about salvation. This means that promises about living as a Christian are not seen as hypocritical, as the parents want their child to make good life choices and reflect these particular values. For some families, a greater emphasis on thanksgiving, blessing and support in the service would be appreciated, and yet some found the thanks-giving service disappointing, lacking the depth and gravitas of baptism. The symbols, movement and drama of the baptism itself emerged in the research as the most important and memorable moments of the service, and will speak for themselves. Any symbolism or action included will add to the significance, so make the most of the drama afforded by the liturgy.

Responding

There might be around 100 guests at a christening, and for those leading the service a real difficulty can be the mismatch in engagement between the parents and those they have invited to the service. Parents may have deep-seated feelings about faith, and be coming to the baptism with a whole raft of semi-articulated thoughts and feelings about blessing, making good choices in life and belonging to a community and faith. However, it is unlikely that they will have said any of this to their friends. Their guests will have been invited to a christening, which includes a church service – and it can definitely feel that the service is simply filling time until they can get to the real business of the day. Yet these people are in our church, and most of them will be aged 18–40, a diverse age range with which the Church of England finds it hard to make contact.

Whatever the guests look like or are wearing, it is important to remember that they are guests of the family who have brought their child to be baptized. The Church of England is not the arbiter of taste to the nation, and I remind myself when I raise a mental eyebrow at certain people's choice of clothing that they will be raising an eyebrow back at a middle-class, middle-aged woman of fashion (that's me!). It may be that many guests have little or no previous experience of church attendance, and don't realize that they are taking part in something, rather than being spectators.

Once the main baptismal actions are complete, people return to their seats and the congregation will respond to all that has happened. There will be a welcome, perhaps applause, and then some words inviting people to join in with prayers. This is one of the best opportunities in the service to do something imaginative, which engages everybody present.

I first tapped into this when I was speaking at the christening of a friend's granddaughter. This was in Sunday morning worship and most of the christening guests were church-confident. It happened to be Epiphany. Linking together the journey and the gifts, I handed out tiny parcels to everyone in the congregation. At the beginning of the intercessions I invited them to open the gifts, and there were lots of surprised smiles as they discovered that each parcel contained a baby sock. I invited them to hold the sock as we prayed for the child and the journey she was beginning, and for those who support and lead children and for children in the world. I then said that if anyone wished they could keep the sock and use it as a reminder to pray for this child and the children in their lives. I was quite surprised that there was not a single sock left behind.

A few weeks later I was leading a different type of christening. It was a stand-alone service in the afternoon for a young couple with family connections to church but no current churchgoing activity. The place was packed with around 100 of their friends and family, most of them young adults. I had decided to give the 'prayer socks' just to parents, godparents and grandparents, which worked really well, but I found I had quite a few little parcels left. I told all the congregation of the idea, and said that if they wanted they could take one from me at the door. I could not believe how many of those young men and women took a 'prayer sock' parcel, and I soon ran out.

It is not always possible to buy and wrap 100 baby socks – but there are other ways of achieving the same purpose. For example, a simple prayer bookmark (see www.churchprinthub.org) could be handed out to guests as an invitation to pray for the child. It can include contact details for the church where the baptism happened, as well as information about where they can light a candle online as a prayer. Experience shows that if such a card is left in the pew, it will not be taken away, so it's important to explain and hand out such things confidently. Those present then know what to expect, and how to take part.

Life Events

There are lots of other ways of involving the congregation in prayer. Another idea that has worked well is to give everyone present a blank luggage label as they arrive. When it comes to the prayer, invite them to write their name on one side, then hold the card as the prayers are led for the child who has been baptized. After prayers have been offered, collect all the labels in and place them in a little box (perhaps creatively decorated with the child's name and date of baptism by one of the regular congregation) and give it to the parents, reminding them that this contains the names of all the people who prayed for their child that day. People might also be asked to write prayers on a gift tag or other card, perhaps for a prayer tree or station in church. This can be quite difficult to do, though. It can be hard to know how to articulate the range of thoughts and feelings experienced at that moment, and for some writing itself may not be easy. (These and other prayer ideas can be found at churchsupporthub.org/baptisms/ideas.)

Over and over again during the research around life events, and during the pilot phase in parishes, prayer turned out to be a way in which those who may at first glance seem a long way from a journey of faith can be engaged and involved. It is one of the great gifts that God has made available to all of us, and there may well be a secret life of prayer flowing more widely than we will ever realize. But it is good to remember that research is about patterns, not predictions, and even with the best creative ideas, the warmest smiles and the support of the congregation, sometimes there will be services where it feels like nothing has worked. That's when it is useful to remember that we just don't know what impact has been made, what seeds have been sown, and where life might flourish in a different place and on another timescale.

What about communion?

Sometimes baptism takes place in parish communion, which for those with little familiarity with church can seem a difficult service. A few respondents in the research mentioned that they found sharing the peace awkward (but that is not just those unfamiliar with church!) and were unsure of what was expected of them. At this point in the service, once the event the family has come for has happened, guests sometimes take the opportunity to leave; they may have looked at the time and then at the service booklet and made a calculation of how long it will continue. Much of what has been said earlier about warmth, explanation and keeping things relevant can help. For example, one thing that parents mention as being particularly special is when the vicar, or perhaps an older person from the regular congregation, holds or carries their child. This could happen during the sharing of the peace, connecting that child into the wide family of God's people.

It may be helpful to be very clear about the fact that everyone is welcome to come forward for a blessing, but those who are unfamiliar with church may prefer to remain in their seats, perhaps watching what is happening. In a growing Pentecostal church I visited recently, there was an area near the back with sofas and coffee tables where those who are just edging their way in, perhaps unsure about being there, can sit during the service. There are always a few people around to sit with them, make a coffee, answer questions – and if they want to go outside, that's fine too. It made me reflect on how sometimes we just need to let people be in the unfamiliarity of church, and not worry too much about how much they take part to begin with. There may be an opportunity later to talk further, answer questions, or just simply reflect the joy of the occasion.

Going out to live with joy

In the last part of the baptism service, whichever type it is, the child is given a lighted candle – everyone is sent out to live the life of Christ in the world. The giving of the candle emerged as one of the most significant moments in the service for baptism families, seen as personal and special. The idea of shining as a light is a powerful image that is easily understood: the child carryies a light that will be there for the family, and the light of Christ for that child will never leave them whatever life brings. So, even in a baptism with several families, it is a great moment to be as personal and prayerful as possible. It is also a nice touch to invite previously baptized older siblings to bring back their baptism candles, and relight them as a reminder of all it means.

The family will leave the church usually to go to a party, an occasion of joy and celebration. Nothing says celebration like applause, so an opportunity to reinforce the mood and show that we believe the party to be a part of the day can be really positive.We can inadvertently set up a kind of sacred/secular divide, where it seems that we (and God) are involved in church life but are not really part of anything else, so it is great if someone from church can go along to the party, particularly if it is held in the church or village hall. It may be at the party that some of the questions, thoughts and experiences of the guests may be voiced, as the vicar takes time to listen. Among perhaps 80 or so guests there is often a story of recent bereavement or recent joy that needs to be shared, or there may be a question about church practice or a previous experience that can lead to further sharing. It can be the moment when we discover that some family members have an active Christian faith, praying faithfully and living as an example of faith, even when we suspected the baptism family itself of having little familiarity with church. I always find it a joy to discover these friends, knowing that there will be loving prayer surrounding the child as they continue their journey of faith.

The good news of God's love revealed in Jesus Christ is joyful, and as they leave after the service the family are setting out on an amazing journey that will last a lifetime and beyond. It is as they leave that the Church's work begins: our job is now to help them on that journey as we continue to build relationship and help them discover the fullness of life that has been given to them.

'I think the church's responsibility once the child is baptized is to make sure it continues to offer welcome in God's name. Because if there is one thing the church is about, the business of the church or the mission of the church if you like, is to offer hospitality, not just as that entry point for baptism, but through-out the child's life, the life of the family, because what they are doing is having that beginning with Christ, taking the first step, and we need to be there so that we walk the mile with families.' (Vicar, Birmingham)

6 Follow-up makes all the difference

For many clergy in the focus groups, one of the biggest disappointments is the sense that the relationship that has begun to form and the faith journey that has been started can seem to all come to an end on the day of the christening. There is a BBC information film about buying a TV licence that shows a couple meeting, falling in love, marrying, having children, arguing and divorcing all in the space of one 20-second conversation. It has the strapline 'You don't have to do everything all in one go' – and as the baptism service ends, it is good to remind the child and family that this is an event that is to be spread over a life-time. The Church of England is deeply committed to engaging with children and young people, and with the adults who parent them, and we are privileged to be meeting a constant stream of people who make contact with us asking for their child to be christened. So the research was particularly important in finding out how we can best support parents after the baptism, and discovering both what attracts them to come back and what might prevent them.

When we asked parents what stopped them engaging with church after the baptism, the top answer turned out to be surprisingly simple: they didn't know what was happening. One consistent finding across all our research, whether baptisms, weddings or funerals, is that those we have been involved with would like to hear from us afterwards and are often disappointed when we are not in contact.

'I don't think I have heard from them since the christening ... It would have been nice to have a little reminder they are still there.'

Although many churches do try to maintain good contacts, sending out items such as parish magazines and newsletters, it is very easy for those to be ignored or dismissed.

It seems that the type of follow-up that makes an impact and actually feels as if the church is staying in touch is much more invitational and focused. Since we began to present these findings, a number of parishes have been approaching follow-up with families in a different way, particularly around key festivals. One vicar in Blackburn sent all his baptism families special invitations just to the crib service. He didn't send them a list of all the services on offer at Christmas, but simply chose the one that was especially aimed at families and children. He talked of his surprise at seeing people queuing to come into church on Christmas Eve – with several of them clutching their invitation as though it were an admission ticket. This experience resonates with the research:

'I felt I had now been invited to church and could go on a Sunday and people would accept me.'

It may seem strange to those of us who are actively engaged with church, and can barely remember a time when we didn't feel at home there, to think that people don't realize that church services are public, and you don't need an invitation to come along. An invitation makes people feel as if they have been included in something and therefore they belong. I remember consistently sending invitations to families for our monthly 'all-age service', and being surprised at the way people would stop me in the local shop to tell me their intentions, apologizing if they couldn't come but clearly feeling that they had been included.

Churches can lose confidence quite quickly around keeping in touch if they don't see people at a service after a couple of attempts at making contact. The research showed us that if the church where the baptism took place kept in touch, this was influential in encouraging families to go to church wherever seemed best for them at that time. The experience of the baptism itself was very strongly seen as positive, with around two out of three feeling that they were now interested in going to church at least to a small extent. However, the depth of the relationship that had been built before and during the baptism influenced the strength of that expectation. Those who had felt fairly distant from church, and were generally more negative, were much less likely to have any sense that they had been encouraged to continue with church after the christening. The follow-up is a continuation of the relationship that is already being built.

Respondents were asked whether there was anything about the church that had encouraged them to think about churchgoing in the future. The most important factors were about relationship and welcome, and an impression that the vicar and the church were friendly and likely to be interested in families.

> *'All of the people we invited said what a lovely service we had and that the vicar and congregation were extremely friendly. I think this really encourages people to continue to attend church who may not otherwise.'*

Families were also asked whether they had found anything off-putting or discouraging, but the number of respondents choosing any factor was very small. The top reasons were again related to friendliness and warmth: for example, feeling that the church is not for 'people like me' or that the actual christening service was impersonal. The reality is that we are not doing anything to push people away – however, we are doing little to pull people back towards church. That sense of being drawn back begins with realizing that we are interested enough to keep in touch and invite baptismal families to specific activities.

Family-friendly occasions

The occasions that families might be interested in attending may be different from those the church expects. The number one time when baptismal families are likely to return is around Christmas, but other invitational opportunities might include Harvest Festival services or even Remembrance Sunday. Harvest Festival has gained an increased importance in urban as well as rural contexts, particularly where schools celebrate harvest, often linking it to environmental stewardship or justice issues. Major charities such as Christian Aid or Tearfund produce materials specifically aimed for use with children and families around harvest, so it could be a good time to invite families specifically. Remembrance Sunday has also grown significantly in importance over recent years, and some of our respondents referred to it as a time when they like to take children to church. Uniformed organizations are often involved, and the idea of a service largely taking place outside, involving marching, music and colour, as well as silence and solemnity, can be appealing to families.

> *'When there are special services we always try to make sure we go to them. So when they do like services for Remembrance Day, then normally it will start a bit later, so we do try to go to them.'*

Other opportunities for families to feel part of a church community might be a summer fete or Christmas fayre, a family quiz night or a community action day. All these can be times when parents and children can build the kind of relationship that means they feel a sense of belonging.

> *'Since the christenings of my sons we have attended more things at the church, not necessarily attending services, but family events such as Christingle, May Fest, Harvest Festival and supported and attended spring and summer events they have held in the village. We definitely feel more a part of the church now, than we did prior to the christenings!'*

Other special events in the church year you could invite baptism families to might include a Christmas tree festival, or an Easter egg hunt. It is worth noting that Mothering Sunday – or Mother's Day – might need to be approached differently with families. The day is now largely presented as a 'treat your mum' day, with things like meals out, breakfast in bed and special visits high on the agenda. Going to church on Sunday morning may not fit easily with all of that – so inviting children and families before the day to prepare and to pray might be an effective approach.

This is partly because the reasons parents give for not going to church are to do with the pressure on time and whether church is seen as an activity that is a good use of family time. Contemporary family life has become very busy and Sunday morning is often the only time when a family can chill out a bit, get up late, stay in their 'jammies' and watch movies together. For other families it may be a day for hobbies, interests and sports, with drama groups, rugby, football, swimming and lots of other demands on an already busy schedule. Increasingly, keeping in touch with family and friendship networks is complex – there may be several sets of grandparents to visit, arrangements with different parents, friends from university living in different towns, and all of this has to take place at the weekend.

> *'I quite enjoy it [church] – it's just on Sunday morning my son has swimming lessons … Sunday is the only day my husband gets off work, it's a family day really …'*

Parents with a first child are busy working through the complexities of a major life upheaval and will often need to prioritize sleep, whereas parents with several children are caught up in the need to fit in the older ones' activities as well as finding time to be together.

One church thought carefully about how to build a family congregation. They started a 'creative church' once a month at 4 p.m. on a Sunday afternoon – many churches have found this to be a good time to engage with families. The interesting thing was how they worded the publicity – 'Let us give you the gift of time to be together as a family.' There was a real sense that for two hours on a Sunday afternoon there was an opportunity for the family to be together plus the space to be involved with activities that are not always easy to organize in modern family homes (the UK has some of the smallest homes in Europe).

The amazing journey: Ministry around the baptism of a child

Child-friendly churches

Organizing a church service that is different in feel from regular Sunday morning church may help in addressing another set of concerns expressed by parents, which is that church is not child-friendly.

Being honest, this is often true in all kinds of ways. As a physical space it can be quite difficult, with access that may be awkward for buggies and possible lack of toilets. The building may be cold or damp and full of trip and bump hazards such as steps, stone floors, candles, jutting edges and so on. It is not easy to bring a baby or toddler into this space. And that is before we think about the emotional energy required to enter a space where the expectation has been inbuilt for years that you must be quiet and behave.

I am still haunted by a Sunday service where a mum, baby and two-year-old came in just as the service began. The already harassed mum followed the elder child to her choice of seat – right in the front row. The service got under way and all went well until the two-year-old began to protest – probably because Mum had just said 'no' to something interesting like walking up the nave to look at everyone. The wails got louder and the woman became more stressed, which meant that the baby she was holding also began to whimper and then cry. No one was worried. I smiled sympathetically, but eventually she made the decision that she had to leave and walked out of church. No one followed her. With hindsight I wish I had stopped talking at the front and simply gone to reassure her, but sadly she left and as far as I recall never came back. Quiet and church have been intrinsically linked, and however much a congregation tries to be empathetic it can feel like a huge hurdle to bring a toddler into the space.

> 'At the age that he is, all they do is put toys down, and there isn't any other babies that go at his age, so all the older ones go off to the children's group, but he goes into like a little play area, and there's only one other little girl, that's sort of his age ... when I take him out, we're not really doing anything that's really church.'

As parents shared their difficulties in coming to church, they often added the intention that they would come back when the children are older. There are a number of key moments throughout childhood when life habits and interests get reassessed. One of these will be when the child starts at nursery and begins to engage more intentionally with other children and with a range of activities.

Life Events

This is a good time to get in touch with parents and make sure they know about any toddler or other groups your church hosts or organizes. But in relation to attending church itself, this is most likely to be revisited about the time a child starts full-time school at around the age of five.

Many churches have a well-established practice of sending anniversary cards each year to remember the date of a child's baptism. Mothers' Union members are often involved in this, and cards are available to send for as long as a church wishes. At every event we speak at, we always ask how long people send cards for, and there are usually at most two or three, if any, who send them for longer than three years. Yet if families rethink their churchgoing habits when a child is 'older', keeping in touch into school years could be really important. It might also be that this is a great time to offer practical pastoral support. I know of a couple of churches with premises en route to local schools who offer tea and tissues in the first week of a new school year. After that heart-stopping moment when your little one (hopefully) runs confidently into the classroom, emotional parents can pop in to share stories. A prayer tree or similar space could also provide an opportunity to ask for God's blessing on the new stage of life's journey.

How to keep in touch

The incredible statistic that has emerged across all our research is that fewer than one in ten parents didn't want the church to keep in touch. Two-thirds of those who were involved in church post-christening expected that the church would be in touch with them – and they were. Invitations to specific events are all-important, but for many parents it is also helpful if we can give them some real practical insights into what it means to live out the journey of faith day to day. There was evidence in the research of a clear desire for life to have a spiritual dimension, even if going to church was felt to be near impossible to achieve.

'I still won't go to church any more often than I did. But it has made me think more, when I'm doing things with my daughter, trying to teach her values and being a good girl and things and I do think, well, she's been baptized now, and instead of getting cross with her I should be sitting there trying to be good and calm and maybe … It's made me think I've got to be a better person, I've started her on this journey. Sometimes I think that when you go back and have

a ceremony it makes you think, you're not being a very good person today and you're not being a very good mummy, you've got to sit down with her and be a bit more patient and practise your Christian values, not just say, I'm faithful and I'm a Christian, and then get cross and be mean to people. Sometimes at work I do that as well, I think you're not being very Christian to the customers today, because you're sort of nice to their face and then go out and do this, and then I think, well, that's not very Christian, so that has made me think ...'

Offering parents ideas about how to pray with and for their child, what Bible stories to read and simple ways of living out values of love, hope, joy, kindness and generosity could all be helpful. 'Next Steps' is a newsletter that parents can sign up for (see www.churchofenglandchristenings.org) that is full of simple and ordinary ideas to encourage parents on the journey. Much of the content is also available for parishes to download and use themselves in their own communications with families, however that happens. Increasingly, communication needs to happen in a number of different ways, although it has always been a marketing truism that people need to see information at least seven times before they take action.

Real mail, using the post, is still very important, especially for invitations. No one ever prints out an email and props it up on the mantelpiece (even if they have one), or even sticks it on the fridge. Emails stay in the inbox to be referred to later if needed, or deleted or ignored.

Most post that arrives is impersonal, so a personally addressed envelope stands out and attracts attention. But that will only be one of the ways to keep in touch with families.

E-newsletters are really helpful. Although email is no longer the preferred method of personal contact between people, it is still well used by organizations, businesses and charities to keep in touch with members. Most of us have email inboxes that reveal all our tastes and interests – mine is full of newsletters from various clothing outlets, travel companies, theatres and organizations such as the National Trust and National Gallery. They send these out, perhaps monthly, perhaps seasonally, and they will keep on sending them until I choose to unsubscribe. There is no one sitting in an office worrying that perhaps as I haven't actually visited the gallery for a year I may not really be interested, and maybe it's a bit pushy to keep sending me things. They just keep in touch because there will come a day when everything fits together and I do actually go along to something. There are practical tips about developing an e-newsletter on the Church Support Hub (churchsupporthub.org).

Social media is also really important, and Facebook in particular works well to build both awareness of an activity and a sense of community. Create a Facebook group for your activity and engage with it, updating the page regularly; it is amazing how quickly it becomes a place of belonging as well as information. I recently did this for a monthly family activity, and never cease to be amazed at the interaction that follows, especially when I post photos. There are many more tools out there that can be helpful in communicating and keeping in touch. If it feels daunting, ask around until you find someone confident who can help you get started.

What are they coming back to?

If the Church wants to take seriously the possibility that families who bring a child for baptism are beginning an amazing journey of faith, discovering all that it means to live in a relationship with God made possible in Jesus, then it may be that we need to think about what is on offer to families. We have already seen that the most important reason given for not coming back to church is simply a lack of awareness, followed by a sense that it is not a good use of precious family time and that it may be more appropriate when children are older. We can perhaps make church more accessible by thinking about practical things like time and place and the physical welcome of the space.

In one village, there were several families with young children, but the church was a really unsuitable place for toddlers and small babies – damp and cold with no running water or toilets. I have noticed that in very small communities (this one had a population of less than 300) there are often cohorts of babies around the same age, followed by fallow years with no new arrivals. It was decided to hold a short service once a month in the home of one of the families; then, as confidence grew, other families offered to host the event.

For some churches, developing new initiatives such as Messy Church or 'Little Church' have been helpful in engaging with families:

'I take her to a creative Church, the last Sunday of every month ... Basically it's like arts and crafts for children but with a biblical meaning behind it. I think everyone else there will have something to eat afterwards but usually we have

plans on a Sunday, so I'll go to the service and do the arts and crafts, but usually we leave after that. But it's quite a good way of getting families to go to Church. It's good for kids, because sometimes you struggle for things for them to do ...'

But starting a whole new programme will not be realistic for many, and it may be that a few changes to the way in which the church engages with children and families can really help. It is important to keep reminding ourselves that above all else it is the 'soft stuff' not the 'hardware' that makes the biggest difference: families in our research were drawn by relationship and care for their family rather than repelled by particular unfriendly or unrealistic church services.

When I worked as Children and Families Adviser I set off one afternoon for a field study tour of how different churches welcomed children. What I wanted to do was see what kind of impression a family would gain of how seriously the Church takes a child's spiritual journey. After six visits I was so depressed I had to go home. It seems that while every church had an area that was called something like 'children's corner', in reality these areas had turned into what I renamed 'dead teddy corners'. They were heaped up with old soft toys and other tired games and playthings.

Yet we are introducing children to a relationship with the God who made the universe, who created the stars to shine, the spiders to spin webs, the sunlight to sparkle. We are introducing children to the wonder of possibility and the amazing truth that God is interested in them. We have the incredible stories of the Bible to explore – from Miriam dancing to Samuel listening, and all of Jesus' wonderful life to discover.

The quality of offering for children and families can reflect the reality of our expectations about their participation in the amazing journey of faith. There are so many wonderful opportunities to explore God's world, whether literally, as many pre-schools and nurseries do by spending time outside, or by providing items that reflect our spiritual life. Lots of ideas on how to do this can be found on the Spiritual Child Network (www.spiritualchild.co.uk) and similar websites. In the early years we are all beginning to work with the building blocks of our spiritual lives, discovering awe and astonishment, mystery and wonder. The children's author Michael Morpurgo writes in his memoir *Singing for Mrs Pettigrew* of the importance of early discoveries and play that can lead to a lifelong sense of delight in the world. Our children's areas can reflect some of these qualities.

Worship that everyone, regardless of age and ability, can engage with is also part of the offering that helps to make church attractive to families. There are many things in our culture that communicate simultaneously with audiences at different ages without 'dumbing down' or being patronizing, and many books with ideas about how to develop worship where everyone has the possibility of an encounter with God (for example, *Worship Together*, SPCK, 2012). Key factors include involving senses and movement, engaging with mystery and wonder, building strong patterns that create a sense of belonging and sharing stories that are relevant to all grappling with the big issues of life, at whatever age.

Ultimately people become part of a worshipping community because, as one respondent expressed it, 'It's where we find our friends.' That isn't necessarily people all at the same stage of life but a community of people who are interested in the lives of those around them, often crossing age boundaries. Young families may welcome friendship with older people, and many older people miss grand-children who live far away. Bridges can be built and friendships can be forged. And through all of that the great friendship with God through Jesus is lived out.

Conclusion: It's an amazing journey

'Can I book a christening?' It's a deceptively simple question. Yet it offers an immense opportunity to explore the good news of Jesus Christ and open up something truly exciting. I think I am most down-hearted by the research respondent who said, 'I do believe in something … it's just not what the church says.'

I'm down-hearted because it seems that we have fallen short of sharing the dynamic, exciting nature of a relationship with God through Jesus and instead given people a static experience which they can rail against. But the experience of the Life Events work around the baptism of a child under 12 has been that a few simple shifts in thinking and practical tools can make a huge difference to baptism ministry in any church, large or small, urban or rural, which means that we can share the joy of discovering the amazing journey of faith. The key words that emerged from all the research are confidence, courage and relationship, and they apply to ministry with the families who approach us at the life-changing moment when a child arrives in their family. My prayer is that we will have the courage to take the opportunity, build relationship and have confidence in the gospel and the work of the Holy Spirit! The same core principles apply across our ministry to wedding couples and bereaved families, so read on to discover more.

SIX KEY MOMENTS ON THE AMAZING JOURNEY

Here are six key moments when a church who wants to become confident in ministry to baptism families can take action that will make a difference. It starts with prayer, and then moves through the opportunities for contact to the christening itself – and into the future.

1 **Pray** – talk with the regular congregation and ask individuals to begin praying specifically for named baptism families, offering a card to remind them each day.
2 **Publicize** – let young families in your area know that they can ask about a christening or a thanksgiving service with posters and leaflets.
3 **Inform** – at the first meeting, give parents appropriate information to take away and remind them of what it means to have a child baptized at a christening using a leaflet and a web address card.
4 **Celebrate** – use baptism preparation to celebrate friendships and relationship, especially godparents, giving them a thank you prayer card to share.
5 **Involve** – on the day itself, welcome everyone with a smile and include them in prayer for the child, using a prayer bookmark or other creative idea.
6 **Invite** – send specific invitations to Sunday worship or seasonal celebrations with details of your church and your services.

TOP TEN THINGS TO PUT INTO ACTION

Alongside the moments of contact, there are changes in thinking and approach to families that can help to build relationship and enable people to have a positive encounter with God and God's people. These ten tips are based on the research and the experience gained from parishes over the past few years.

1 **Use the language of christening** and remember it's a celebration for both family and church community – answer enquiries with a smile in your voice.
2 **Talk with parents** about their faith journey and experiences, including their

memories of church in childhood and other life events they have marked in church.

3 **Share the wonder** and the worries of parenting and learn to translate these into spiritual thinking.

4 **Review your approach to baptism preparation** and think about doing something different, especially if it brings people together.

5 **Invite families to church** before and after the service so that they can meet 'people like us' who worship there.

6 **Big up godparents** – contact them, name them, thank them, honour them in the service and plan to celebrate with Godparents' Sunday.

7 **Use names in prayers** and **give the symbols drama** during the service.

8 **Involve everyone at the service** in praying for the child using creative ideas and approaches.

9 **Send invitations to specific church activities and events** rather than just dropping round a magazine.

10 **Involve the whole people of God** in praying and blessing specific baptism families.

Part Three

The promise of love: Wedding ministry

There was no bridal procession, but a sudden silence fell upon the room as Mr March and the young couple took their places under the green arch. Mother and sisters gathered close as if loathe to give Meg up. The fatherly voice broke more than once, which only seemed to make the service more beautiful and solemn. The bridegroom's hand trembled visibly, and no one heard his replies. But Meg looked straight up into her husband's eyes, and said, 'I will!' with such tender trust in her own face and voice that her mother's heart rejoiced and Aunt March sniffed audibly …

They stood watching her, with faces full of love and hope and tender pride as she walked away, leaning on her husband's arm, with her hands full of flowers and the June sunshine brightening her happy face – and so Meg's married life began. (Louisa M. Alcott, *Good Wives*, 1868, Chapter 2)

There is a timelessness about weddings that means that although these words were written nearly 150 years ago the thoughts and feelings, relationships and celebrations feel very contemporary. In the early years of the twenty-first century, weddings and marriage are as life-changing as they have ever been, even if the customs and practices that surround them have changed dramatically. Deciding on a lifetime and life-changing commitment that will establish a new social and familial unit is a major life event, and the Church of England has been part of the changing world of weddings and marriage for centuries. It was in response to one particular change that the Archbishops' Council decided to investigate some of the motivations and experiences of couples who have a Church of England wedding. From that research, the Weddings Project developed resources and insights that have helped parishes approach wedding ministry differently over the past few years.

The particular change that prompted the original research and fresh interest in wedding ministry was the 2008 Marriage Measure, which introduced the concept of 'qualifying connection', giving couples a much wider choice of churches to choose from when they decide on a church wedding. The full story of that research and the work that emerged can be found in Gillian Oliver's *Church Weddings Handbook*, and for those who have never engaged with the Weddings Project, this is recommended as an excellent resource to start churches thinking about this ministry.

In this part of the book, we will reflect on research and developments since the original Weddings Project presented its conclusions, and also recap on the key moments that emerged from that work as significant points of contact for couples. In Part One of this book three key themes were identified as having emerged from all the research and thinking that has been done about the Church's mission and ministry at life events over the past few years – confidence, relationship and courage. These three themes are also part of the story about Church of England weddings. Here we reflect on how these words relate to the Church's contact with wedding couples, and examine wedding ministry in the light of the broader research about life events.

A changing market

Since the original research for the Weddings Project was undertaken the UK weddings scene has continued to change, with new trends and expectations emerging as to what a contemporary wedding should involve. The number of weddings in England and Wales continues to fluctuate, but there is no longer a major decline in marriage. However, the statistics show major changes in who gets married and where they choose to hold the ceremony. It is no longer the norm to be married in one's early twenties – first marriages are now happening in the mid-thirties, and the fastest growth is happening in those over 50. However, many marriages in that age group are not first marriages, but second or even third, and this has implications for the choice of venue for a wedding ceremony.

There are more venues than ever to choose from, and TV programmes such as *Don't Tell the Bride* (Channel 4) feature weddings that happen in special or unusual locations, although the actual legal part of the ceremony has to take place inside a permanent building. Those wedding ceremonies that take place on football pitches, underwater or in the midst of the sky dive are not the legal part of the occasion, but increasingly couples are happy to accept that there may be two parts to the day – the legalities and the celebration. In 2013, over 70 per cent of all weddings were civil (as opposed to religious) weddings, a percentage that has grown consistently since the mid-1970s. By 2013, 85 per cent of civil weddings took place in approved premises, a change that has had the biggest impact on the weddings market since it was introduced in the 1990s. In 2008, 67 per cent of religious ceremonies were Church of England weddings, and by 2013 the figure was 72 per cent of religious ceremonies, a small but significant increase.

Although many other venues are now available, the Church of England continues to meet thousands of couples through wedding ministry each year, with an opportunity to talk to around 90,000 people (45,000 couples) who are arranging to get married in a church. In addition, each of these weddings will bring further contact with the friends and family of the bride and groom. Anecdotally, there is an indication that the size of congregations at weddings is slowly increasing as opportunities for celebration take on more importance. An average wedding congregation may be around 80, with many of them being in the age range 18–45 and whose contact with church on other occasions may be very limited. Although guests at a wedding are there to celebrate and support the bride and groom, there is still an amazing opportunity to ensure that they leave with a positive experience of the church. Many young adults will go to lots of weddings over a fairly short time-frame – one such couple I was speaking to recently, currently in their twenties, have attended weddings for eight of their friends in the past 18 months. It is important that their experience of church is just as memorable as any of the other ceremonies they attend – and for the best reasons.

Before exploring the insights and practical resources that have been developed to support wedding ministry, the next section takes a look at how Jesus was involved with weddings by reflecting on the story of the wedding at Cana.

Biblical reflection: Jesus and weddings

The original Weddings Project team spent some time reflecting on the Scripture around weddings, and in particular the occasion when Jesus himself was a guest at a wedding – the story of the wedding at Cana is found in John 2. We continued to look at this Scripture as our research and thinking developed, and three important themes emerged.

- Jesus himself was a guest at a wedding, taking part in the hospitality and festivities on offer – he was part of the event, sharing in the sense of celebration that might well have been going on for days.
- The actions and presence of Jesus transformed the situation from one that might have been awkward to one of abundance and delight. One of the most striking things about the miracle is that the wine that was poured was the best wine – even though by this stage the guests would probably have made do with something cheap and cheerful!
- We have no idea what happened next – whether any of those present, including the couple, became followers of Jesus. The generous miracle was simply a blessing to those who were present that day, although later reflection revealed a much deeper significance for some. The theological purpose of the story is made explicit in John's Gospel when we are told that the sign is to reveal to us something of the true identity of Jesus as the Christ, the Messiah.

Within the contemporary Church of England, each wedding gives us an opportunity to be present at a moment of serious joy, to witness to the presence of Jesus that transforms the ordinariness of life into something extraordinary, and to do so in a way that reflects the unconditional generous love of God. It is about reflecting the warm hospitality of God, shown through words of blessing and welcome and supported by prayers for and with the couple.

It is in the context of weddings that Archbishop John Sentamu has spoken about Christ as the host, and each person present as a guest (see *The Church Weddings Handbook*, chapter 5 for further reflection).

I was raised in Uganda, where the church was not the vicars or those who attended. The church actually belonged to God and we come to that church as guests of Christ. Christ is the host. We are his guests. We are his friends. And Bishop John V. Taylor, who was shaped by his work as a missionary in Uganda, said that actually, Christ calls us together to make him visible. So the job of a vicar, the job of a parish is to be that kind of community that is so open to friendship. When it comes to weddings, it isn't your church in which they are getting married. It is the church of Jesus Christ, where all of us are guests. (Archbishop John Sentamu, Weddings Project, 2010)

Confidence in wedding ministry

It was very clear in the original research around couples' experience of church weddings that the Church of England's confidence around wedding ministry is rooted in two things: first, that the way we conduct weddings is seen as excellent, and second, that those who come to us asking for a church wedding are spiritually serious. Both of these findings have been echoed in our subsequent research around funerals and the baptism of children, where we also found that those who come to us report having a good experience, and their motivation is often much deeper and more complex than we may initially realize. The Weddings Project discovered that, without exception, couples had positive memories of their day in church, consistently rating the day as 10/10 – this is explored more fully later in this chapter. Perhaps more importantly was a fresh insight into what might motivate couples to choose a church wedding, and also what prevented them from asking for one. A greater awareness of motivation and fears can help the Church of England to be more confident in encouraging couples thinking of being married to talk with their local church about how we can help them at this key moment in their life.

Lost in translation?

The Weddings Project research discovered that the language couples often use to express their deeper reasons for having a church wedding may not be the language that the Church uses to talk about spiritual matters. Words such as 'proper' and 'traditional' carry a weight of meaning, expressing the implication that the ceremony goes beyond the events of that day, placing the story of this couple alongside the greater story of God's love and faithfulness. It is the seriousness of the vows that can only be used in a church ceremony that conveys this, alongside something about the history of the place. There is a clip from one episode of *Don't Tell the Bride* where the bride and her mum are shown walking around inside their local church, trailing hands on pews, and talking about what a church wedding would mean to them:

> 'For me, it's not about your wedding, this place. It's the essence of the place, it's the feel of the wood, isn't it? It's just a calm, a calmness that comes and

descends. The true essence of marriage is promise in the eyes of God to one another. Nowhere else can that happen. It's gotta be in the right place.'

I remember talking to one couple, Caty and Craig, about why they wanted to get married in their local church, and I wrote about this in a blog for the Church of England (see churchsupporthub.org/article/wedding-talk). Craig said:

'If we are going to get married, it has to be in church, otherwise there is no point.'

As we chatted further, we talked of stories and histories, and of his sense that the Church is a witness to good and positive things. For Craig, a civic venue didn't resonate with layers of meaning in the way his local church did, standing testimony to the faithfulness and goodness of God (although he didn't use that specifically religious language). Listening carefully to the spoken words and to the body language used by couples as we meet them can give real insights into that deeper thinking, even if it is only tentative. Sometimes people mask the importance of what they are saying with embarrassed laughter, dismissing any idea that they might be serious. They might cover their mouth with a hand, revealing that they may actually be less than confident in how we are going to hear them. This may lead to a lack of confidence from couples even in asking whether they are able to be married in a particular church, local or elsewhere, with a real fear as to whether their request will be responded to positively.

Outreach and reassurance

There is still a lot of confusion and ignorance about how to go about organizing a wedding in a church, and whether or not any particular person is eligible. Families will talk about whether they are 'allowed' to marry in church, and language around permission and qualification may add to this sense of uncertainty. There are opportunities for us to become more outgoing as we try to address people's fears and also share some of our confidence in the special service that is available through a Church of England wedding.

The Church of England's wedding website (www.yourchurchwedding.org) has become the first port of call for thousands of couples in the eight years since it was launched; it was rebuilt in 2015 to be usable on mobile phones and tablets, easy to navigate and with clear information. It is built around the questions and anxieties that couples face as they begin to plan their special day, and also contains lots of practical information to help them with everything from legal questions to choosing readings and involving children. Most couples who call a vicar or church office will already have looked at this site. The site encourages couples to talk to the vicar of the church where they would like their wedding, explains how they might make a connection, answers worries about having to be christened if you want a church wedding (still a common misunderstanding), as well as explaining what the day itself might involve. However, there is still a need for the Church to offer more information and advice, particularly for those who may be further back in the planning process, and one of the best places for us to do this is at local and national wedding fairs.

The majority of those who attend wedding fairs may already be some way into their wedding planning process, and be busy looking for dresses and cars and cakes and confetti, but some visitors will be newly engaged and just beginning to dream of the perfect day. They may not even have realized they can ask about a church wedding, so our presence at the fair, with appropriate information available, is really important. Being on a stand at a wedding fair is a wonderful opportunity to witness to God's love, and perhaps to challenge perceptions of the Church of England. Many of these shows take place on a Sunday, so at a local level this may mean working together as a deanery so that a small team can be released for this valuable ministry. It is a great opportunity for conversation, and to discover that we can have confidence in who we are and what we do.

At the National Wedding Show we often ask couples if they would like us to pray for them on their wedding day, regardless of where the wedding is taking place, and many of them are delighted with that offer. In 2016 we gave away a beautifully presented gift of a 'prayer candle' – a lovely gold tealight in a special box with a prayer saying simply:

Loving God, bless us as we plan our marriage. Amen.

Only a handful of couples refused this gift. It was offered regardless of the type of wedding they were planning – church, civil or overseas – and met with a warm response. As I spoke to one couple the bride's eyes began to fill with tears. She explained that they so needed the reminder about being married, adding that in the stress and expectations of the wedding show they were already arguing and losing sight of what it was really about. I realized that in the whole of the 200 or more stands, we were perhaps the only one featuring the 'M' word – marriage, not simply a wedding. Prayer is one way we can support all couples as they plan and prepare. (This candle gift is now available as a resource for local churches to use – see www.churchprinthub.org.)

The joy of wedding fairs

Making sure that we give clear, accessible information not just about the process but also the particular joy of a church wedding is really important. This might mean giving away the Wedding Pack or a simple leaflet called 'Just Ask', which encourages those who are uncertain whether a church wedding is for them to find out more (both available from www.churchprinthub.org). A local wedding fair is a great opportunity to hear what couples are concerned about, discovering why they might not be choosing to have a church wedding. Increasing numbers of couples are choosing to get married abroad, so there is an opportunity to talk with them about a 'blessing' service when they return. Others are anxious to have everything in one location, and it is the journey from church to venue that puts them off – but that journey may well be the only part of the day that the couple can be together, something they may not have considered.

Some churches have begun to host their own wedding fairs. In one church this was combined with an exhibition of wedding dresses from across the decades, accompanied by the stories of those who had worn them. This gave the event a very warm and personal feel, enabling potential church wedding couples to come in and discover more, and see how their story would become part of the wider community story in that place. Others have brought together church musicians, soloists, florists, local photographers and bakers into the church venue to highlight the way in which a church wedding can include as much or as little of the traditional elements as a couple wish. Sometimes churches are able to showcase local or church facilities as reception venues. One couple, who were planning a wedding on a budget, were delighted to discover that the local village hall was the best option for their reception – and it was only a short distance from the church! As the local church realizes that we can be confident that a church wedding is both meeting real needs and offering a service that is special, so we can grow in confidence in telling others about all that we offer. This might also mean sharing stories, for example, using local media opportunities, whether regional magazines or social media forums.

Building relationship

Wedding fairs can give rise to all kinds of questions, and open up all kinds of opportunities. I was working at the National Wedding Show at the NEC in Birmingham when I met Trish and David, who were very serious about a church wedding but didn't know where to start looking. They were wondering whether they could get married in Gloucester Cathedral. I was able to explain the particular circumstances that apply to cathedral weddings, and encouraged them to visit the parish church close to the cathedral where I sometimes help at Sunday worship. Imagine my surprise when they turned up!

I went on to take their wedding 15 months later. This church is not near to where they live, and is not in a particularly picturesque location, but having chosen to be married there they began coming along to church in the year leading up to their wedding to establish a connection under the Marriage Measure. Many of the regular Sunday congregation were present at the wedding, and everyone joined in their excitement. Family members accompanied the couple when the banns were read and on other special occasions such as Mothering Sunday. I was helping out with a bouncy castle at a cathedral family activity recently when Trish and David came in specially to talk to me. They were glowing – which meant it was fairly easy to guess their news! They had gone out of their way to find me and tell me that within a few months, all being well, there would be a new member of their family. The next day they were planning to go to the church where the wedding took place to tell the congregation their good news. They belong – and that's why they want to share their good news with me and the Sunday congregation.

This openness to relationship is very important, as the way in which we make friends with couples is at the heart of their experience of a church wedding. The Weddings Project research discovered that for the couples the most important person is the vicar. It is the vicar who will guide them through the church wedding process, and the vicar who will stand with them on their wedding day as they make their vows. In a civil wedding, although a couple may meet the registrar who will conduct their ceremony when they go to make the booking, there is not the same sense of personal connection as will emerge through contact with the vicar. One of the biggest changes that has emerged since the inception of the Weddings Project is the extent to which relationship is forged not only with the vicar but with a local congregation as well. This has happened as a direct consequence of the Marriage Measure 2008 and in some circumstances the need to establish a connection through regular attendance. When a church is open to the possibility of saying 'yes', even when the reason for choosing that church seems to have little to do with location beyond the proximity of the venue, then the possibility of building friendships and inviting them into the community is opened up.

One such church lies in the picturesque village of Bourton-on-the-Water at the heart of the Cotswolds, which is surrounded by a plethora of attractive venues for wedding receptions. It is not uncommon for couples to travel to the countryside from major cities – particularly London and Birmingham – to find their venue, and then they find the local village church. The vicar and the PCC have a policy of saying yes to enquiries if they possibly can, and this means that couples are required to attend church for at least one Sunday a month for six months before their banns can be read. One such groom, travelling regularly from London to be at this church, emailed the vicar, sharing his thoughts about all that being present at the service had come to mean:

> *'I've been telling lots of my friends about my church experience and how much I look forward to the service you lead and also the opportunity to spend an hour in quiet contemplation of the week gone, the week ahead and life in general … Often life is so fast-paced with friends it's hard to find an appropriate moment to discuss spiritual inclinations or your view on matters that move away from the standard mundane [sic] of work, food, mortgage, etc.'*

Experience has shown that couples will attend church in order to establish qualifying connection – but then an amazing opportunity opens up to show something of the hospitality of God and the love of Jesus reflected in the way they are welcomed each week. The experience of being at church becomes a part of the story of their wedding planning and their marriage preparation.

Weddings ministry: Moments that matter

The Weddings Project identified seven key moments on the wedding planning journey of any couple (see page 102), beginning with the **first contact** – often a telephone call or perhaps an email. Or it may come through a web enquiry or even a Facebook message, and the relationship we build begins with the response to this; just as became clear from the research around baptism, whoever answers that first enquiry needs to respond with the right note of congratulations, warmth and possibility. The Life Events team deal with lots of enquiries from those who need information about how to go about organizing a wedding or a christening, and every reply will include words of congratulations and prayers for their future, which is a gentle way of expressing the love of the God who is interested in them and their lives.

The Weddings Project identified the second key moment as the **first meeting with the vicar**, one that couples may approach with real trepidation and anxiety, fearful of rejection and judgement. This apprehension (called the 'white coat effect' in medical circles, where blood pressure rises just because we are at the surgery) can come across in a number of ways. They may use language that equates church with every other aspect of their wedding planning, talking about booking the building, questioning details, demanding particular things. But over the past decade of hearing from couples who have later queried some aspect of their wedding planning, we have realized that this anxiety may lead to them not always coming away with clear information, often hearing words given as advice or a suggestion as actually forbidding something. One couple were seriously worried because the vicar 'said' they couldn't have a guitar playing for their entrance music, but in reality the vicar had simply been trying to suggest that guitar music may not fill the church space in the same way as organ music does.

To help fill some of these gaps, the Weddings Project produced a lovely pack of information, presented to look like a gift, which is much appreciated by couples. This has been updated to reflect both legal and cultural changes, and, based on feedback from clergy, includes space for the local church to insert their own information sheets. This provides an opportunity for the church to give details of local resources such as bellringers and flower-arranging, and list details of worship and other activities that happen in the faith community (available from www.churchprinthub.org).

Where a couple need to establish a connection through attendance, then following on from the meeting with the vicar will come the important moment when the couple first meet the congregation. Although the contact with the vicar remains at the heart of the planning, there is now a role for the whole people of God in wedding ministry. This a major difference from the emphasis in the original Weddings Project, and means that there is now a specific way in which wedding ministry becomes a ministry of the whole people of God in a particular community.

There are lovely stories from across the country of how couples have felt welcomed and included by the local congregation. One couple chose a village church because of its proximity to their reception venue, and began to travel monthly to attend worship, not just in 'their' church but in other churches across the rural benefice. One Sunday when they were attending the news was announced of the death of a much-loved long-time congregation member. The bride talked with surprise of how she felt emotional herself at the news, realizing that they themselves were becoming part of the community. On the morning after their wedding, this couple went along to the local church to thank the congregation for all the help they had given to them, help that had been both practical and personal as the months went by.

The importance of welcome is one of the fundamentals that has emerged across all our research: if we are going to make the most of the opportunities to meet people at key moments in their lives then the whole congregation needs to become outward-looking, taking on the responsibility for building relationship. Even if couples are not establishing a connection through attendance, the vast majority will have an opportunity to attend church to hear the **banns being read**. The research showed that for many couples this remains a special moment in their wedding journey, and gives a valuable opportunity for the church to make contact, especially with those who may live in their parish but having a wedding elsewhere. It may be that the bride and groom attend together to hear their banns read, or perhaps just one of them along with a parent – who may be the one living in the parish. It is easy to overlook the potential of a renewed relationship with the family around the couple, and yet they are often the ones who are living in the local parish. The following story illustrates the importance of this occasion in one woman's spiritual journey:

> *Paula is in her late sixties. She is a regular and faithful member of the congre-*
> *gation who hardly misses a Sunday. Paula came through the doors of the church*
> *for the first time nine years ago. Although she had been baptized as a baby, she*
> *had rarely been to a church service anywhere in her adult life. She came that*
> *morning to hear her son's banns being read. Paula would be the first to tell*
> *you that the only reason she came that day was because she had been asked to*
> *do the flowers for the wedding and she wanted to count the pews so she could*

count how many pew ends she would need. Coming to hear the banns read gave her an excuse – permission if you like – to come through the doors. Something stirred in Paula. She came the next week for the second reading and the following week for the third reading and she continued coming week after week until the wedding itself was a distant memory. The banns experience changed Paula's life and in due course she was confirmed. She is now an active PCC member. She is part of the Messy Church team. She is in church most Sundays and if she misses a Sunday, chances are she will be there at the midweek Communion instead. Paula's story is not unique. There are others in the congregation who are there because some time in the past they came to hear their own banns being read or they came to support sons and daughters having their banns read.
(Sally Lodge, Proceedings of General Synod, February 2017)

This echoes the findings of other research, which has discovered that going to church and attending a service is one of the most important ways in which people are drawn onwards in their discovery of all that the good news of Jesus can mean in their lives. A very valued part of reading banns is offering prayers for the couple – this enables the whole congregation to feel that they are supporting this couple and is much appreciated if the couple are present. It may be appropriate to offer the wedding prayer candle or a simple card at this point to remind the couple of the support and care of the church community where their wedding will be held. Even if a couple don't make it to church to hear the banns read (and the pressures on time and family in the last few weeks before a wedding may mean that the best of intentions don't translate to action), then letting them know that they are being prayed for and thought about may be greatly appreciated.

A further opportunity to build relationship with couples comes when churches offer **marriage preparation**. The weddings research discovered that neither clergy nor couples are completely happy with this terminology; one title that was suggested for whatever programme or course is offered is 'space to think'. From conversations on the Church of England stand at various wedding shows, it became increasingly clear that the pressure around organizing the wedding day can overshadow the purpose of the whole event – getting married! Taking time to think about the difference that marriage will make to the relationship is really valuable for couples, even those who have lived together for many years. It is also a great opportunity for couples to hear the vicar and other church members share something of their own stories and get to know them, perhaps over coffee and refreshments. The Your Church Wedding website (yourchurchwedding.org) includes some really helpful material about what it means to be married, encouraging couples to look closely at the vows and think about what they will mean to them as they make their new lives together. Even if it isn't possible to organize a formal 'space to think' session, it could be helpful to encourage couples to take some time to look at these pages.

Keeping in touch

The seven key moments identified in the original Weddings Project, extending from the initial enquiry to the first wedding anniversary, are times when the local church has a particular opportunity for contact. This is likely to be a long timespan, and there can be an incredibly large gap between the initial meeting and the next formal moment, which could be either marriage preparation or the reading of banns.

The length of time from booking a wedding to the day itself varies considerably, but for many couples it will be almost two years from official engagement to the ceremony. In the initial excitement of planning, the couple will be booking many things – reception venue, photographer, cake, cars and the church. In the intervening two years or so, each of these providers will make contact several times, reassuring the couple, looking for opportunities to meet them again, and acknowledging the milestones of the year. For example, a hotel wedding venue will send information about Valentine's Day, Mothering Sunday and Christmas, and many will also routinely send an invitation for dinner around the anniversary of the engagement or a year before the wedding (an invitation to spend money, usually, even though it may include a special discount or extra treat such as champagne).

Conversations with couples at wedding shows reveal a lot of anxiety about the lack of contact from their church once the initial booking has been made. After that first meeting there may be over 18 months before the invitation to hear banns being read or attend marriage preparation. Some churches have begun to invite couples to specific occasions during the year, perhaps organizing an event around Valentine's week (though not Valentine's Day itself!) or inviting couples to come to a particular Christmas service. It is interesting to note, when you consider all the other things that couples book as part of their day, that in each case both the couple and the provider have a real interest in them experiencing the product on offer. No one would book a reception venue without having at least a drink there, everyone would expect to sample the type of cake the baker is offering. And yet, both couples and church seem to be comfortable with the idea that you might never actually experience the building alive and awake before the day itself.

The lack of contact and information coming from the church after a booking has been made can become particularly worrying if the parish goes into vacancy during this time. At wedding shows and through other enquiries, we hear about couples who are concerned about who will be taking their ceremony, and whether everything will still be all right. One of the strengths of a Church of England wedding is the quality of relationship with the vicar and with the local church, so although the vicar may be changing, it can be helpful for the church to keep in touch and make sure there is continuity with the community and clear information shared. Many churches use the Pastoral Services Diary (see Part Five), which means that they can keep in contact regularly and easily with all those they meet through life events ministry. This is particularly important with wedding couples where the key moments for contact come over an extended time period, and that might include contacting them when change is happening at their church. For example, one couple discovered at the wedding rehearsal that half the church was hidden behind plastic sheeting as major renovations were being carried out, works that were not scheduled when the wedding was booked. Sending news, whether through regular e-newsletters or special invitations or updates, can help couples to feel part of the community, and strengthen their connection to church.

The final contact before the day itself will be the **wedding rehearsal**, and this is also an opportunity to cement the relationship. There will be members of the wider family to meet – and often they are meeting each other for the first time too. For younger participants in the service, this may be their first ever experience of church, so it's a chance to help them feel something of the warm hospitality of God's people (even if the space is cold!). The wedding rehearsal can also be an opportunity to draw the couple aside and listen to their last-minute feelings, excitement and anxiety. As well as checking that all the practicalities of the service are in place, making sure the details for the register are correct, this can be a time to pray with them, asking God's blessing on them as this special day draws close. I have been taken by surprise by the depth of emotion around rehearsals, particularly where there is bereavement and absence, and a moment of prayer can hold all these feelings.

On the day

When it comes to the Big Day, the Weddings Project discovered that for almost all the couples in the research the wedding service itself was the highlight of the day, and all of them rated their experience 10/10. The Church is good at doing weddings, and contemporary weddings are made special by personal touches that make the day feel unique. The importance of the church being perceived as personal also resonates throughout the research, and is something that stands out as significant throughout our contemporary culture. Good customer relationships, whether in finance, travel or retail, are hallmarked by a sense that the experience is personal. At a Church of England wedding, personal is also very important, although it is not about being able to write unique vows or craft particular words. The marriage service is valued because of the timeless, traditional nature of the vows that are made and the words that are spoken. Couples appreciate that a church service is the only place where those particular words can be said, where rings will be blessed and God's blessing given to the couple.

Individuality can be shown in the choices the couple have made, not just about colours and flowers but about choreography and music. It may be that they want bridesmaids to walk in front of the bride, or the couple to meet at the door rather than at the chancel step, or to have the family dog as an attendant. But the heart of the personal touch emerges in the additional words and actions beyond the liturgy itself. It is in the way guests are greeted at the door, welcomed into the church, and personal stories acknowledged. It is when people go out of their way to help find the right seat for the guest with a broken leg, or help the family with young children find the place where they can see and yet also play. It is particularly appreciated when the vicar's sermon is relevant and appropriate for the couple and their story, and when prayers use names. Details such as lighting a candle to remember a family member who has recently died become very special.

Imaginative ways can be used to help those present pray for the couple: ideas similar to those shared in Part Two on baptism are also suitable for weddings. At a recent wedding service I gave each person a gift tag, and invited them to write their name on one side and their prayer on the other. They were collected up, placed in a jar and given to the couple as their 'support system'. This jar reflected a positive action in response to the question the whole congregation answer earlier in the service as to whether they will support the couple in their new life together. In another service, small heart-shaped baubles were handed out with a tag attached. The congregation were simply invited to hold the hearts as the prayers were led, and write their name on the tag. The glass hearts were placed into a bowl as people left the church, a reminder again of the prayers offered that day. A lovely pew card is available for guests to take away, reminding them of the promise they have made to support the couple in the year ahead (see www.churchprinthub.org). Some clergy have now, famously, gone the extra mile in order to create something special for a couple, with personalized songs and special 'flash' dances, but these will not be everyone's choice. The good news is that personal is still best expressed in smiles, humour, story and kindness, all things that every vicar, helper and church member can offer to a couple.

One of the biggest developments that has happened since the original Weddings Project research has been the emergence of social media as a means of communication and relationship-building. It's hard to believe, but when this work first began in 2008–10 there was no widespread use of tablets or smart phones, and social media apps such as Facebook and Twitter had limited reach. For the generation of young people who are now thinking about marriage these tools are not special or unusual, they are simply the way they communicate in their world. This means that social media can be part of the way in which a church builds and maintains contact during the wedding journey, and also a way of sharing the positive experiences of the day. However, the Church needs to be mindful of how to address the question of the use of social media. In the weddings I have taken over the past two years, couples have specifically requested that a notice is verbally given and included in the service booklet asking that no photos are shared on social media until the day after the wedding. This is so that they have time to enjoy their day, the memories and the images themselves, before it all becomes public. It can be very disconcerting for the couple to discover that even before the ink is dry on the register others are commenting on the experience. But sharing photos and posting congratulations after the day can be a great way of celebrating alongside the couple, and reinforces the importance of this relationship.

The wedding day can be marked by a special congratulations card sent from the vicar and the congregation to the couple, to arrive when they arrive home from honeymoon. It will be there for them as they begin to establish the new pattern of married life together, and provides a link back to the very special day with family, friends and the church, exchanging vows, being blessed and supported.

Courage to continue contact

Sending the wedding congratulations card immediately after the event is the first step to establishing an ongoing contact with the couple. This contact is rooted in the confidence that we do a good job with weddings, and that those who come to us are seriously motivated, and open to hearing about the good news of God's love shown in Jesus. This positive experience is founded on the relationship that is created between the vicar, the church community and the couple, and spills over on the day into the relationship with the congregation – the friends and family there to celebrate with them. It is the strength of this relationship that travels beyond the day, as the Church engages with consistent and sustained follow-up. But for the Church to engage with continued contact will require courage and confidence.

Whether we were talking to parents after a christening or a bereaved person after a funeral, all our research suggests that those who have had contact with the Church at one of life's big moments welcome more contact. Wedding couples also indicated that they would like to hear from the church after the day, and clearly expressed disappointment if they heard nothing afterwards. It may be more challenging to keep in touch with a wedding couple, especially if they are now living far from the church where the wedding took place. It may seem like a lot of effort to send anniversary cards or e-newsletters about the church when a couple have moved 100 miles away and may not visit the parish soon, if ever. Couples who have established a Marriage Measure connection may return to visit for a whole range or reasons – perhaps they have family living in the local community or relatives buried in the churchyard. A card from the vicar may prompt a conversation with a parent or grandparent who lives locally, who may be surprised at how much the Church cares about their child or grandchild. But the Church of England is a national church and although a couple may feel a particular attachment to the specific church where the wedding happened, and to the vicar who conducted the ceremony, there is real merit in keeping in touch so that awareness of church in general is maintained.

There is a specific opportunity to contact a couple on a wedding anniversary, particularly for the first year. The most popular day to get married remains a Saturday, which means that for many couples their first anniversary will fall on a Sunday. Receiving a card with an invitation to come along and an assurance of prayers will link couples with the positive memories they have of a day and a service that was really special. But you could send an invitation on other occasions too, to special services at Christmas or to social events, as well as regular Sunday worship. It may be that continuing to send anniversary cards in future years is also possible, reminding couples that the Church is there to support them in their marriage for the long term. Most of us are now familiar with the idea that organizations like to keep in touch with us, often through e-newsletters, letting us know of new initiatives, activities and events. Those who supplied elements of the wedding day are likely to keep in contact in the years ahead, including the reception venue, caterers and photographer, until such time as the couple decides they no longer wish to hear from them, and unsubscribe from emails and e-newsletters, for example. Even the most trivial of purchases made will generate future contact – so having the courage to keep in touch when we have met a couple through one of the most important moments in their life can make a difference. But we may have to accept the reality that the local church where the wedding took place may not be the one that sees the fruit of this investment of time and resource. It may be years, it may be in a different location, a different denomination, before the prayers surrounding that couple are answered. But we do know from this research and from other research into faith journeys that the positive experience of church and of meeting Christians play a key role in helping people discover the reality of faith in their own lives.

Conclusion: Seven key steps – one important message

Although it is now some time since the original research around Church of England weddings was conducted, the good practice that emerged about building relationship through contact at key points of the wedding journey still applies. We have learned more about being confident in telling couples that we have something good to offer them as they plan their wedding day, and also about the importance of ongoing contact throughout the journey. Nationally, the Archbishops' Council has funded the development of online tools to support parishes in this ministry and produced high-quality printed resources that make a positive impression on the wedding couples who receive them (see www.churchprinthub.org). However, the most important message is not about the resources and the tools. It is that we build relationships with couples that reflect the loving welcome of God, that are reflected in the way we speak to them and about them, pray for them and bless them, support them and serve them as they plan their wedding day and begin their married life together.

SEVEN KEY MOMENTS

The original Weddings Project identified seven key moments with potential for the church to make contact with couples and to build relationship with them. These important opportunities start with the initial enquiry, move through to the special day itself and the first anniversary and beyond. All these are moments not only for getting in touch but also for the whole congregation to pray and support each couple.

1 **First contact** – answer with warmth and congratulations.
2 **First meeting with the vicar** – give the gift of the wedding pack with all the information needed.
3 **'Space to think'** or marriage preparation – send invitation and information as appropriate.
4 **Reading the banns** – an invitation to hear their banns being read and to be prayed for.
5 **Wedding rehearsal** – a special opportunity to cement relationship and build confidence.
6 **The Wedding Day** – send congratulations card afterwards to arrive before the couple return from honeymoon.
7 **First anniversary** – remind the couple of their wedding day and pray for them.

TEN TOP TIPS

Alongside these seven definite opportunities for contact, below are some tips for good practice around wedding ministry. These have emerged from experience and from the research around all the life events, recognizing the importance of confidence, relationship and continued contact.

1 **Say congratulations** – it's a big moment for couples and they are planning one of the most important days of their lives.
2 **Encourage** couples to come along to church and meet the vicar even if they don't need to for connection reasons: after all, they will always go to the reception venue at least once.
3 **Keep in touch** throughout the wedding journey with invitations and information.
4 **Focus on the vows,** which are unique to a Church of England wedding service and are often the reason for wanting a church wedding.
5 **Be flexible** – there are lots of details around a wedding service that are personal choice.
6 **Personalize** whenever there is an opportunity, especially in the prayers and the sermon.
7 **Value guests** by including them in the service, particularly in prayers.
8 **Maintain contact** after the wedding day, sending appropriate information, anniversary cards and invitations to church events.
9 **Pray** for couples on their wedding anniversary.
10 **Publicize** the great wedding stories that happen at your church through wedding shows, social media and community press.

Part Four

With you every step of the way: Funeral ministry

Thine be the glory, risen conquering Son,
Endless is the vict'ry, thou o'er death hast won.
Lo! Jesus meets us, risen from the tomb;
Lovingly he greets us, scatters fear and gloom;
let the Church with gladness, hymns of triumph sing;
for her Lord now liveth, death hath lost its sting. (Edmund Budry)

Yea, though I walk through the valley of the shadow of death,
I will fear no evil; For You are with me;
Your rod and Your staff, they comfort me. (Psalm 23.4, NKJV)

A quick scan on a search engine or of the shelves of any book retailer will reveal the hundreds of books available on the subject of pastoral care for the dying, ethics around death, prayers, and support for the bereaved. Of the three big life events – birth, marriage, death – there is no doubt that the death of someone close has the biggest impact, not least because it is the only one of the three that everyone will experience (notwithstanding we all are born). Facing our own death or the death of someone we have known and loved shapes our feelings, thoughts and spiritual understanding in far-reaching ways.

For centuries, even millennia, religion has played a huge part in shaping the way in which humans respond to death, and in this country, the Church of England has played a huge part in marking the transition from life to death. At the heart of this ministry is the confident proclamation of the gospel, whether expressed in the confidence of the great Easter hymn and the promise of eternal life or in the quiet consolation of Psalm 23, assuring us that whether we are facing our own mortality or living the journey of grief, God's presence will always be with us. This is why we do what we do as we encounter those who are bereaved and those who are dying.

> *'It comes back to the grace of God. It's the grace of God and the gift of God that we're allowed to talk about these things, which spring out of our deep sense of the hope that comes to us, from the resurrection of Jesus Christ from the dead, that gives us that confidence in handling issues around death and dying and funerals.'* (Archbishop Justin Welby)

However, big cultural changes are happening, and over the past 50 years the place of formal religion around death and its accompanying rituals has shifted. It is against the backdrop of a fast-changing culture that the Archbishops' Council's recent research and thinking has emerged. That research and thinking has informed the development of new insights and resources as we seek 'to proclaim afresh to a new generation' the good news to those we meet with big questions, thoughts and feelings about the purpose of life and the meaning of death.

When this work was first scoped out in 2012, following on from the successful impact of the Weddings Project, it was thought of as ministry at the time of death. It became clear early on that, sadly, ministry at the point of death has become more and more unusual, even though preparing the dying for their death is one of the tasks priests are specifically called to do:

> *'They are to resist evil, support the weak, defend the poor, and intercede for all in need. They are to minister to the sick and prepare the dying for their death.'* (From the service of Ordination of Priests)

The days have gone when a minister of religion would automatically be summoned to watch and wait and pray as a person slipped from life into death. While it is still a core part of the ministry offered by hospital and hospice chaplains, for those in parish ministry it has become relatively unusual. When it does happen it is a deep privilege to spend time with family and friends, to be able to offer a profound experience of God's loving presence. The work and research done has helped us to think about how to prepare people for death in new and different ways within the contemporary context, and also challenged us to think again about the extent to which we minister to those facing the end of their lives.

As well as ministering before death occurs, there is a huge amount of ministry that happens after death. For many, the call to licensed or ordained ministry is informed by a deep-rooted sense that offering pastoral care to those in need, including the bereaved, is of immense importance. Valuable work is done through charities and medical services to help with bereavement, but the support and space offered through a local church still has an important part to play for many families.

At the heart of the charge to prepare the dying for death and offer pastoral care for the bereaved is the funeral service itself. For most families their encounter with the Church of England at a bereavement begins when they make contact with the minister who will lead the service. The work done by the Life Events team takes the funeral service as the starting point, and although there are many other issues that emerge once we start talking about death, this book focuses on the fresh insights that emerged around the funeral itself. It is the opportunity and privilege of preparing and leading funerals that brings us into contact with bereaved families, whether or not they are active members of a local congregation, whether or not they have an active professed Christian faith. This is part of the way that churches serve communities through the work of licensed and ordained ministers and the prayerful support of the whole people of God as they live out their faith as salt and light in their neighbourhood.

> 'Funeral ministry is so important because we are the Church of England, and the Church for England. That's such a privilege, such an extraordinary privilege to be with people at the moment towards the end of their lives, when they're dying, to be with their relatives who've been bereaved. And for me as a parish priest that was one of the most important things I ever did ... The key thing is it's the loving and serving the communities that we are in, and that is at the very heart of the vocation of the Church of England.' (Archbishop Justin Welby)

Findings of the research

The research involved an in-depth qualitative study with families who had organized a funeral in the past year, supported by interviews with leading industry professionals such as the CEOs of large bereavement charities. We did additional pieces of work with funeral directors and held focus groups with around 300 clergy and Readers. From this we developed a series of key messages accompanied by a new range of resources to help parishes, including a new website to help people know more about what a Church of England funeral involves and means (www.churchofenglandfunerals.org – see Part Five for more information). These resources were tested for a year with a further 150 parishes across four dioceses, and during that year ministers shared their feedback. Confidence in what we offer and in the message of the gospel to those who are bereaved was strengthened, new professional and personal relationships were built, and consistent follow-up was established as good practice across those parishes that took part. Five important themes emerged from the research, the insight from parishes and the testing of resources. These are vital to sustaining and developing the Church of England's mission and ministry around funerals and to the bereaved in the changing cultural context of the next few decades.

- The Church needs to be part of the emerging public conversation around death and dying.
- The Church offers distinctive funeral ministry based on pastoral and spiritual care.
- The Church needs to communicate clearly what we offer.
- Building professional partnerships is essential.
- Consistent follow-up and after-care makes a difference.

These themes, which are specific to funeral ministry, together with the over-arching messages that have been reinforced through all the research on life events, will be explored in this section of the book. However, before continuing to explore the insights and practical resources that have been developed to support ministry around funerals, we reflect on some relevant biblical passages from the Old Testament and the Gospels.

Biblical reflection: Widows and orphans

As part of our thinking, the Life Events team, and the wider funerals working group, looked at various scriptural passages, beginning with our reflections on the parable of the sower, explored in Part One (see p. 6).

Some specific thoughts emerged about funeral ministry as we looked at this parable together. Within Jewish culture, there is a mandate to sow seed at the edge of the land so that those who are poorest might come and glean what they need, even if they don't have access to the seed itself. Funeral ministry is one of the ways in which the poorest and most excluded of our society may draw close to the things of God. The Church is often involved with those who die with no family or friendship groups and with little or no financial resources. Increasing numbers of stories have emerged of those who die alone and yet, through social media and the support of a local congregation, hundreds gather at a funeral. In October 2016 the funeral of war veteran Richard Norris attracted huge media attention, when over 200 people who had heard about it through the media turned up at the church in Driffield to be there for this man who died alone. Those who find themselves on the margins of society, such as the travelling community, also can come close to God through ministry around death.

Throughout Scripture the marking of death is recognized, from the first description of a funeral and burial in Genesis 23 through the death of Jacob, of Moses and many others throughout the Old Testament. There is a clear mandate in the Old Testament to take particular care of those who are impacted by death. Within the cultural context of the time this is expressed as concern for widows and orphans, who would have been financially and socially insecure after the death of the male provider. God is described as having a particular concern for those affected:

> *Father of orphans and protector of widows is God in his holy habitation.* (Psalm 68.5)

The concern of God for widows and orphans is reflected in the instructions God gives to his people as to how they should be included within the life of the community. The way in which widows and orphans, the stranger and the poor are treated is a reflection of the extent to which God's people are living God's way (Deuteronomy 12.12; Jeremiah 22.3). Conversely, one indicator that people have drifted from God's ways is their treatment of this group of people, and oppressing widows and orphans brings judgement and condemnation (Malachi 3.5). This concern continues into the New Testament, with the first specific organizational action of the emerging church being to provide well for widows (Acts 6.1), and several encouragements from Paul and the other writers to take particular care of this group (1 Timothy 5).

> *Religion that is pure and undefiled before God, the Father, is this: to care for orphans and widows in their distress, and to keep oneself unstained by the world.* (James 1.27)

Life Events

Being widowed or fatherless in biblical times meant the loss of financial and social status and security, as it still does in many parts of the world. There will be families in England today where the death of a partner or a parent will make a similar impact, even though social welfare systems are designed to mitigate the practical consequences. Changes in 2017 to bereavement payments gave rise to comment that helped underline the impact that the premature death of a parent still has on families. *The Guardian* featured an interview with a 51-year-old husband and father with a terminal illness:

> *His mind quickly focused on the lives of his wife, and their children, a 10-year-old daughter and 14-year-old son, after his death. He feared the 'whirlwind of emotional and financial distress and turmoil' heading towards them as he grappled to draw up a plan. (The Guardian, 3 April 2017)*

Alongside the practical demands of bereavement, the emotional impact remains immense for contemporary widows, widowers and orphans, an issue that is beginning to be talked about more openly. In March 2017 the footballer Rio Ferdinand talked about the death of his wife and how it affected him and his children:

> *I didn't know any techniques to speak to the children. I didn't know what buttons to push. I'd been starting conversations with them to try and get how they were feeling out, and they would just shut me down, walk away, close the conversation down completely.* (BBC News, 27 March 2017)

Shortly afterwards, Princes William and Harry began to speak about how they are still working through the trauma of their mother's sudden death 20 years previously, after suppressing feelings before eventually seeking help.

The Childhood Bereavement Network estimates that 23,600 children lost a parent in 2015 – that is one parent every 22 minutes (see www.childhood bereavementnetwork.org.uk). By the age of 16 around one in 20 young people will have experienced the death of one or both parents, and the emotional, social, educational and life consequences are immense. And many adults in mid-life struggle with the often unanticipated intensity of grief around the death of a second parent, which leaves them 'orphaned'.

Age UK suggest that up to 33 per cent of older people are sometimes lonely, and within that group the widowed are disproportionately affected (Age UK,

Loneliness and Isolation Evidence Review, 2015). The heart of God is turned towards widows and orphans, and God asks that God's people reflect that concern in their response to these groups. For those ministering in the Church of England, the funeral is often the point of first contact.

Jesus and funerals

We then looked specifically at the Gospels to see how Jesus responded to death and funerals.

Although there are a number of places where Jesus encounters death, we soon realized that we had a problem: Jesus himself never took a funeral. Instead, when he appeared the funeral and burial arrangements were somewhat disrupted! There are several examples, but the one we looked at most closely concerned the raising of the widow of Nain's son, found in Luke's Gospel:

> *Soon afterwards [Jesus] went to a town called Nain, and his disciples and a large crowd went with him. As he approached the gate of the town, a man who had died was being carried out. He was his mother's only son, and she was a widow; and with her was a large crowd from the town. When the Lord saw her, he had compassion for her and said to her, 'Do not weep.' Then he came forward and touched the bier, and the bearers stood still. And he said, 'Young man, I say to you, rise!' The dead man sat up and began to speak, and Jesus gave him to his mother. Fear seized all of them; and they glorified God, saying, 'A great prophet has risen among us!' and 'God has looked favourably on his people!' This word about him spread throughout Judea and all the surrounding country.* (Luke 7.11–17)

The unusual thing about this story is not that there was a funeral happening that day in Nain. Funeral processions would have been commonplace, happening every week, as this was a culture where life was precarious and death could strike at any age and stage. The presence of a large crowd following the bier was also part of normal cultural practice when a person died, one still common in large parts of the world today. Accompanying the dead is part of identifying our common human experience, and also showing compassion and care for those who remain. It is not unusual that Jesus has compassion on the woman. Sometimes this story is used to encourage us to follow Jesus' example in showing compassion for the bereaved, but in fact Jesus is simply doing what is right and expected of him as a good Jewish teacher and leader. He is reflecting God's compassion for the widow, and this is yet another sign of his authority and religious observance. The unusual things start to happen in verse 14. The first of these is that Jesus touches the bier – under the law (Numbers 19.11), anyone who touches a dead person is defiled and unclean for seven days. But then the really unusual thing happens: the dead man sits up and is raised to life! And Jesus restores him to the widow, which probably redeems her social and financial prospects as well as restoring joy into her life.

The final unusual thing about this funeral is the impact it has on those around. The actions of Jesus at the funeral lead people on in their understanding of just who this man might be, and the news spreads once more.

In my many years' experience of taking funerals, I have never yet failed to complete one because the dead became un-dead (although I know that there are parts of the world where such things are reported as still happening). So as we reflected on this passage, there was a clear idea that emerged: the presence of Jesus transforms funerals. Jesus changes the funeral from an occasion of despair into an occasion of hope. It is this that underpins our ministry at funerals, as we speak of the transforming presence of Jesus and hold out hope to those who are bereaved, acting with compassion and without fear in the sight of death. Funerals also have an impact in the wider community – news that the message of hope has been shared spreads, and people are drawn to question and think about the person of Jesus, and taken onwards in their journey of faith.

Although the context for contemporary funerals is changing, and the opportunities for ministry may be different, good funeral ministry can be a really important signal to a community that God is with them, and that God's people care for them. Shortly after I arrived in one parish, the tragic death of a 16-year-old girl happened. The response to that death, the funeral itself, and the relationships that followed were so important in the unfolding ministry over the next few years. Many clergy talk of how ministry around death, funerals and bereavement is pivotal in their relationship with the community, particularly at the beginning of ministry in a new location.

However, the cultural context in which we minister has seen many changes over the last few decades, not least around death, dying and funeral ministry, and the pace of change seems to be accelerating. The next section examines some of these changes.

Cultural changes and demographic realities

The last two decades have seen major changes in the possibility for the Church of England to meet people at this most important of life's key moments. The biggest shift began with the emergence of independent funeral celebrants during the 1990s. I was ordained in 2000, and even in north London we weren't really talking about celebrants at that point. But by 2004 the Institute of Civil Celebrants was formed as 'the result of the need to drive up the quality of funeral ceremonies in the UK. Its aims are to further the provision of Civil Funerals and support the work of Civil Funeral Celebrants' (www.iocf.org).

The emergence of a real choice about the nature of the funeral ceremony available and who could lead that occasion has had a direct impact on the Church of England in particular.

In 2004 the Church of England conducted just over 200,000 funerals; by 2016 that figure had fallen to 139,000. This is a direct consequence of the emergence of options that are becoming increasingly important in a culture where religious adherence is changing. The other shift that has had a real impact is the decline in the numbers of people who choose to have their remains buried rather than cremated. Although the first legal cremation took place in Woking in 1885, growth was slow until after World War Two. In 1957 the one hundredth crematorium was opened in the UK, in Salford. By the year 2000, there were over 240 crematoria in the United Kingdom and over 70 per cent of deceased were cremated.

Since 2000 there has also been a major growth in the use of woodland or natural burial grounds, and there are now over 270 natural burial sites in the UK, although the types and standards vary hugely. The growth of choices means that there is a great deal of information available about the different types of funerals, and this, together with a decline in awareness of what the Church of England offers, has had a big impact on the opportunities to offer the kind of ministry that has been helping people for generations.

We have given some thought to the language used here to describe funerals where the Church of England is involved. Throughout this book, and in the leaflets and websites produced as part of the national work around funerals, the term used is church-led funerals, as more than half of these take place in locations other than church buildings.

It is still the case that around one-third of all deaths in England are marked with a Church of England-led ceremony, which brings us into contact with a huge number of people. There are wide regional variations in these figures, with highly urban and diverse areas such as the Diocese of Southwark involved in a much lower percentage of funerals, whereas rural dioceses such as Carlisle will still be involved in marking the majority of deaths in the area. The number of 'close' or 'warm' contacts (outlined in Part One) is difficult to quantify when we talk about those we meet through funerals. I have been involved in organizing funerals where there have been no friends or relatives to meet, and have also walked into a living room for the funeral visit to be confronted by around 15 people.

Mortality statistics show that the most likely circumstances in which we will be involved with a funeral are for a person aged 75 or over. It is an intelligent guesstimate to take three as the number of people usually met at such a funeral visit – perhaps a surviving spouse and two adult children or grandchildren. Meeting three people at each funeral visit with whom we have the opportunity to have a conversation potentially gives the Church of England contact each year with around 450,000 people, or an average of around 9,000 people each week.

Again, it is almost impossible to calculate the numbers of people who have the opportunity to have contact with the Church of England through a funeral led by a licensed minister, whether in a church, crematorium or cemetery chapel. Funeral attendance can range from a handful – or even no one – to several hundred. As congregations at church funerals are not included in the statistics for mission, and congregations at crematoria funerals are not even counted, this figure is also a guesstimate. But based on a sensible average funeral congregation of 50, the Church of England may have contact with around 7.5 million people each year through this ministry.

Missional moments: The story of 'Fred' and 'Linda'

Each person who attends a funeral brings with them their own story and their own journey of faith. As those leading the service we have no idea whether people are very close to God or very far away, or whether this is the first funeral they have ever attended or the latest in a series. For older people, there may come a season when attending funerals becomes much more frequent, as acquaintances, friends and colleagues of the same age face their own mortality.

This is a typical story of a couple in their sixties, reflecting on the contact they might have with church during the course of a year.

Fred and Linda lived next door to Betty and John for around 30 years, the couples helping each other out at different stages of life. Sadly, Betty died at the age of 80 and Fred and Linda found themselves at her funeral, led by the local vicar at the crem. Although not a religious person, or a regular churchgoer, as he sits in the service Fred finds himself remembering the funeral of his colleague, Andy, who died suddenly aged 62. Ever since then Fred has become really conscious of his own mortality, and wakes up worrying about the future, about what he has achieved, whether his family are all right, and what his own funeral might look like. As for Linda, whenever she goes to a funeral she always remembers the day 35 years earlier when she buried her stillborn child.

Over the next year Fred and Linda find themselves meeting vicars in different places for different occasions – they go to a family wedding in the summer, then their granddaughter is christened, a good friend's mother dies and they go to the church to support her, and they find themselves back at the crem for the funeral of the local pub landlord. At Christmas, Linda encourages Fred to come with her to a carol service – it feels like a space where they can think about everything that has happened. She has also taken to popping into the large town-centre church to light a candle and sit for a bit with her thoughts.

I don't know when the right person will come along and invite them to draw closer, ask them to 'come and see', perhaps through a social invitation or a special event, and it may be that they continue to journey towards God on their own. But throughout the Church of England countless people touch something of the good news of God's love in Jesus Christ through the services and support offered around funerals and bereavement.

Death: The ultimate certainty

The cultural and technological changes of the last few decades are set to continue and proliferate as we progress through the twenty-first century. But one thing remains certain: death. One of the key reasons why funerals and all the related services and products are of great interest to both commercial companies and institutions is simply because it is the one universal market. Since the early eighteenth century people have been quoting – and misquoting – the saying that the only thing certain in life is death and taxes. These days some people seem to find ways around one of those, but as yet no one has found a way to avoid death.

The influence of the 'baby boomers'

Unlike the other two major life events – births and marriages – we know that the absolute number of deaths in England will increase significantly over the next 20 years. This is directly related to the age profile of the UK population. There is a significant growth in the numbers of over sixties, as the generation known as 'baby boomers' are reaching the last major life stage. This 'bulge' in the population demographics happened in the post-war years 1945–55 when there was a massive increase in the birth rate. Since then, as this cohort has moved through various life events, there have been corresponding increases in statistics, so that weddings reached a peak in the 1970s and there have been subsequent mini-booms as this generation had children, then grandchildren. The increase in the death rate will be gradual because of continued longer life expectancy and improvements in health and social care, but the absolute number is on the increase.

Much has been written about the baby boom generation in terms of characteristics, but hallmarks have included a questioning of authority, a desire to do things 'my way', individualism and a decline in the place of institutional or organized religion, yet an increase in the spiritual. As one person expressed it to me: 'The generation that invented Woodstock is not going to go gently into that good night.'

One important factor about this cohort, alongside the increase in numbers, is that they are leading the changes that we are seeing around funerals. These characteristics are now being reflected in the way in which funeral ceremonies are being shaped, including in some cases the desire to have no ceremony at all – as happened at the death of David Bowie in early 2016, himself part of the baby boom generation.

Ministers talking about funerals

The research took place against this backdrop of the importance of funerals ministry but a decline in opportunities to meet people at this point of need. Conversations with clergy and Readers in focus groups revealed just how valuable funeral ministry is in local communities. Over and again, ministers spoke of the privilege of being entrusted with the stories, emotions and questions that arise when death becomes part of life. One vicar talked of hearing secrets that had never previously been told and of the sense of responsibility that comes when faced with trust and vulnerability.

Ministers have a real sense of pride in funeral ministry – this is a task that can be done well for a family at a point of real need. It is often an area of ministry for which vicars and Readers are thanked specifically. Many recall receiving cards over the years that acknowledge how helpful a funeral service has been on the person's bereavement journey; the sense of finishing a task and knowing it has been done well is important. In parish life clergy and others are engaged in work that may continue without any sense of knowing whether anything is being achieved, so the occasional recognition is appreciated. This contributes to a quiet confidence for many that Church of England funeral ministry is being done well; however, in every group there were stories of 'rogue ministers' or difficult colleagues, some of whom had not accessed training around funeral ministry in a long time.

Alongside the positive feelings there are real worries about funeral ministry. These are wide-ranging and include anxieties about balancing day-to-day administration with the awareness of the need for pastoral care. 'Follow-up is desirable but not practical,' said one minister, reflecting the tension between the desire to be in contact with bereaved people after a funeral and the pressures of parish life. Some of those in rural ministry, where there are still significant numbers of funerals in church, feel particularly stretched by ministry over several communities.

However, by far the biggest concerns expressed were around the role of the funeral director in the process. There were so many different comments and views. Sometimes this was expressed as, 'The funeral directors have favourite clergy,' but more often it was about the way in which funeral directors are perceived to either limit or open up choices for families. This is such an important aspect of funeral ministry that a whole section of the research was concerned with this particular relationship (the insights from this are discussed on p. 151). Going beyond the immediate worries, clergy and Readers also identified the pressures that have emerged in the changing cultural context, where there is now a real choice as to how the needs of the bereaved are being met now and into the future.

'They [funeral directors] can do it all without us. If we disappear funerals will still happen and pastoral care will still be given.' (Vicar, Blackburn diocese)

Although that statement expresses a deep fear, the Church of England offers much that is distinctive and different around funerals. The research showed that the message of hope and the depth of experience that ministers bring is still widely valued, as well as some very specific opportunities and challenges for the Church of England as we continue to reach out with a message of hope for the dying and the bereaved. The Church of England has some key opportunities to engage with the new culture around death and funerals and the demographic changes that face us. As we listen to the messages that emerged from the research and utilize the resources that have been developed, there is a strong sense of building on current and past funeral ministry to find a new way forward that remains faithful to the heart of God's concern and to the good news of Jesus Christ. There are no simple solutions, but as the public conversation around death, dying, funerals and bereavement becomes more audible, sharing our insights and experience may be a place to begin.

The in-depth qualitative research conducted on behalf of the funerals team helped us to develop fresh understanding about how the Church of England's ministry around funerals is experienced and perceived both by those we help and by those with whom we work professionally. This led to the five important themes identified earlier, each of which are explored in depth below.

FIVE KEY INSIGHTS ON FUNERAL MINISTRY

1 The Church needs to be part of the emerging public conversation around death and dying

There's a leaflet lying on my desk just now. It's attractive and glossy and advertising an exhibition at Bristol Museum and Art Gallery called 'Death: the human experience' that was held in late 2015 to early 2016. The exhibition included some of the museum's death-related artefacts, and there was an accompanying series of talks about death and dying. It concluded with a 'Death Fair' on the last day. This exhibition won an award for the 'Most Innovative Death Public Engagement Event' at the 2016 Good Funeral Awards. It's not the only such festival to have taken place around the country – others have been held in

Cambridge, Cardiff and the at the South Bank Centre in London, for example – and it reflects one side of the strange dichotomy of attitudes we face about death. Writing about death in the post-modern world, author Ewan Kelly argues that we are living with two contrasting approaches. On the one hand, there is an incredible denial of death, whereas on the other there is a clear emerging conversation about death which Kelly calls 'the revival of death' (Ewan Kelly, *Meaningful Funerals*).

In some ways people are comfortable talking about death – happy to make jokes or to be open about the challenges faced by a serious diagnosis or to empathize with bereavement. But when it comes to facing and talking about our *own* death, something shifts. We do not want to admit that we ourselves are mortal beings and that the one universal truth about each of us is that we will die.

A great deal of public noise is made about how to avoid or delay death, whether through diet, exercise, activity, taking a certain medication or avoiding another, and so on. Death is nearly always presented as the worst outcome, and as death is pushed out of the domestic environment into the institutional world of medicine we become less and less familiar with the reality.

But there are clear signs that this taboo is being pushed. The death festival is one such sign – another is the emergence of mainstream documentaries such as *My Last Summer* (Channel 4, June 2014) and national initiatives such as an annual 'Dying Awareness Week', coordinated by the Dying Matters Coalition, founded in 2009 by the National Council for Palliative Care. The Church of England and other faith organizations are among the 50 members who support the initiative. In 2016 BBC *Breakfast* devoted a whole week to discussing death and related matters. There are comedies that laugh at death and funerals, articles in magazines, and an increasing number of 'death cafés', featured in various radio programmes since 2013. Daytime television includes lots of adverts for funeral plans and even funeral directors, encouraging people to make sure that they can afford the funeral that they hope for. Yet, less than 15 per cent of people have actually written down anything about the kind of funeral they expect, although our research interviews showed that people are aware that it is something that would be helpful.

'Jay would know what to do anyway, if I die first. But it's one of those things: "Oh, I should tell her about it, let her know." I've thought about it a few times

and "Oh, I'll mention this" but I never do. It's something you should talk about. We have talked about bits and bobs but … it's something you should discuss really. I don't want her saying, "Would Lee want that?" At least she'd know one way or the other, even if she didn't agree with me. Make it a bit easier for who-ever's burying me.'

We discovered that although people sense that talking and planning their death and funeral ahead of time will make it easier for those who have to organize it when the time comes, there is still a real reluctance to engage with it. However, there was also evidence that getting a group of people together to talk about things could be a good idea.

Talking about death

Death Café in England was developed in 2011 by Jon Underwood and Sue Bartsky Reid, based on the ideas of Bernard Crettaz (www.deathcafe.com). They felt very strongly that it was healthy for people to talk about death and to make plans. It is very much a grassroots movement, initially meeting in homes and centred on refreshments with a group discussion. It is explicitly non-religious. The emergence of such a movement is again evidence of the interest being brought to the subject of death and funerals by the 'baby boom generation'. *Mystic Moon* is a canal boat owned by Sue Brayne, author of some key books around mid-life, death and grief, and she moves around England, mooring up in different places, and holds pop-up 'death cafés'. In her first blog for 2017 she shares part of a conversation from one café:

'Life is like a wave,' said someone else. 'It follows the law of physics, and every-one's life has a beginning, middle and end to it.' 'Can you imagine if life never ended?' said someone else. 'How ghastly that would be. Everything would just fall apart. We need to know there will be an ending to value what we have right now, and to give our lives structure and meaning.' We all agreed with this, and it was a poignant moment for the pop-up Death Café to conclude. (www.sue brayne.co.uk/2017)

When the funerals team first explored the concept of the 'death café', we realized that hospitality, space and talking about death was something that the Church of England could be at the forefront of offering. From these initial thoughts and reflections, we developed the concept of 'GraveTalk', which is a specific tool enabling churches to host café space conversations.

'GraveTalk': A new way to talk about death and dying

The church hall was dotted with six or seven small tables covered in pretty tablecloths, with small vases of flowers on each table, and plates of gorgeous home-made cupcakes. A couple of smiling volunteers were dispensing teas and coffees from the kitchen, and another helper encouraged people to sit in groups of four to six at each table. To one side there was a large table with lots of information about the practical issues to do with death and books about grief. In the corner was a prayer tree, with a heap of heart-shaped tags and some pencils nearby.

The host welcomed everyone, and explained that on the tables were 'GraveTalk' question cards. All they had to do was choose a question and start talking. If they ran out of conversation, they could choose another. But there was no pressure to get through a specific number – whether one question took the whole hour or a group talked about 15 topics, it didn't matter. Once conversation started, it was hard to stop. There were bursts of laughter from some tables, and quieter moments when a box of tissues was passed across. The questions cover five broad areas:

- **Life** – what makes it special for you?
- **Death** – memories and experience.
- **Society** – how our culture deals with death.
- **Funerals** – what happens and what could happen.
- **Grief** – the reality of loss.

This was piloted with around 40 parishes in Lichfield diocese in 2014; the pilot was evaluated in partnership with the University of Staffordshire and was well received (see 'GraveTalk Summary', downloadable from churchsupporthub.org, for a full report). We moderated some of the questions and the presentation, then launched nationally during Dying Awareness Week 2015 with a giant café in Portsmouth Cathedral attended by almost 300 people over the course of a day. GraveTalk was featured on BBC *Woman's Hour* in September 2016 as an example of how people are being encouraged to talk about end-of-life issues, and one of the great things about the interview was the mixture of laughter and tears (you can listen to it on churchsupporthub.org/article/gravetalk-radio-4s-womans-hour).

GraveTalk is not about bereavement support, although inevitably during a GraveTalk event people share stories of life, love and loss. It involves creating a space, offering refreshments, and giving people questions (there are 52 in all) to start a conversation. It is about conversation, and not a course – there are no correct answers. But many churches are finding this a great opportunity to hold some deeper conversations, whether people have strong beliefs or many doubts. It is a practical way of helping people to prepare for death, encouraging them to work through feelings and make practical plans.

Within the culture outside church, Death Café and similar initiatives continue to spring up. More festivals are planned, but sadly the Church is often not present in this emerging conversation. The discussion is largely without reference to any organized religion, and so without any of the huge amount of the insight and experience that the Church of England and other faith communities can bring to the table. Sometimes this is because of a reluctance within the Church to take part in such discussions. One person, hearing about GraveTalk, tweeted the idea. Her non-church followers replied, 'Great, when is it happening?' Her clergy friends responded with, 'That's really weird. Why would we do that?'

The public conversation around death and dying is clearly getting louder, and the Church of England has an opportunity to be part of it. At a conceptual level we should be at the table, sharing our skills and insights and offering an alternative narrative and fresh perspectives. At a practical level we need to help people make their funeral wishes known, by talking about their thoughts and then writing them down. At a GraveTalk event there will be information about all kinds of practicalities around death and funerals, and this may include book-lets that allow people to note down their wishes within a Christian framework. People are routinely offered this opportunity when they are sold funeral plans through the large funeral director chains and other financial organizations. As they take out an insurance plan that will mature when they die to pay funeral costs, they are also asked to note down what they want that funeral to involve – but often the opportunity to have a minister officiating is not mentioned. This is something that may potentially have a very big impact on the opportunity for the Church of England to engage with funerals in years to come, which is one reason why it is important that people are encouraged to think about the kind of funeral they and their family will find most appropriate. Many people do want to have a sense of hope and may wish to place the story of their own life within a bigger context, the context of God and the Christian gospel, but unless they have made a note of this, it may not happen.

Thoughts about death and dying

Although our research conversations were primarily focused on people's expectation and experience of funerals, it was inevitable that during the in-depth interviews, people would also talk about death itself. Drawing on those interviews and conversations with other professionals, particularly in hospice care and chaplaincy, we noticed four themes that emerged when people talked about how the person they knew and loved had died. First, people talk about the communities they belong to – family, work or various social groupings. Second, they talk about who they were with when the death happened. Third, they describe where they were, and finally, they identify just how the death happened. One such description was shared by a widow from Bristol:

> *'After he retired he took to going to the pub for a pint in the evening. He came home as usual. He sat in his chair, I was sitting where I normally sit doing some sewing, and that was it. He was gone.'*

This woman's husband was part of a social community at the pub, he was with her in their home – and death happened suddenly. Part of being confident in holding conversations about death, dying and funerals is being able to feel comfortable in listening to these stories and noticing what is important to those who tell them.

In a similar way we also heard people talking about what is important around their own death, again conversations echoed in wider research.

- People want to be treated as individuals – and this is something that is important as older age approaches. People may enter residential care, and for some there may be few friends or family to recall the interests and delights that helped to shape a unique life. A friend of mine was the point of contact for an elderly neighbour admitted to hospital. The hospital called her saying that the lady was in great distress and they couldn't calm her at all. My friend knew that this lady had been a classical ballet dancer, and that every single day of her life had been lived to a soundtrack provided by Radio 3. My friend suggested that playing the right music might help, and it did, for a while.

- We want to approach death without pain, or at least with pain that is manageable.
- The vast majority of us would like to die at home, or at least in familiar surroundings. However, 47 per cent of deaths occur in hospital, and a further 21.6 per cent occur in residential care homes (which may have become 'home' in older age), and only 23 per cent of us die in a private residence. Hospices account for less than 6 per cent of deaths, but often they will be working to enable people to die in their usual place of residence. Statistics suggest that around one in four deaths happen suddenly, without a prior period of illness (see www.endoflifecare-intelligence.org.uk). This reinforces the importance of having conversations with people about life and death matters, whether they are in residential care, in hospital or still living independently in their own home.
- The final factor mentioned is that people express a desire to die in the company of friends and family. Being able to keep vigil at the bedside of a loved one can be a real blessing, giving opportunities to share memories, express feelings and give comfort. However, many of us will be able to recall a story, from either our own or another's experience, of how after watching and waiting for hours, someone finally suggests that we take a break because 'nothing is going to change', only to hear that shortly after we left the room the person 'slipped away'. Being aware of these issues may be helpful if your church wants to begin a ministry around death and dying that includes holding conversations such as GraveTalk as well as individual discussions.

2 The church offers distinctive funeral ministry based on pastoral and spiritual care

Over the past few decades there has been increasing choice, for both families and funeral directors, as to who might conduct a funeral ceremony taking place outside of a church building. Funeral directors are also now training their own staff to lead ceremonies, and for families who have no church experience but who want a personal service that reflects the life of their loved one this can be a good choice. But Church of England-led funerals that share a message of hope in Jesus Christ are distinctive and special, and the research explored the particular factors that underpin this distinctiveness.

Listening well

The building of a pastoral relationship with a family starts from the very first conversation, which will usually be over the telephone when a time is arranged to make a visit. In the training available for independent or civil celebrants a good deal of time is spent on practising and developing practical listening skills at the heart of the visit. Listening well is supported by noticing things about the physical environment – the cabinet full of trophies, the certificates on the wall, or perhaps the person who doesn't contribute to any discussion but is always in the kitchen. Sometimes it is about body language as much as the words that are said, and this ability to listen well is the foundation on which a good funeral is built. For celebrants it is particularly important, as the telling of the deceased's story is the essence of the funeral service. For church ministers, listening well involves not only hearing the life story but also finding out the spiritual needs and expectations of the family.

Practical concerns

It is important that the visiting minister has a good understanding of what is involved with a funeral, not simply what happens at a ceremony. The family will have met with the funeral director and the minister will be the next professional they encounter, and there may be questions that have occurred to them, sometimes practical, sometimes revealing deeper pastoral needs. For example, I remember the teenage granddaughter who was extremely anxious about how she could be sure that it was her grandmother in the coffin. As ministers we need to be confident in our ability to answer or respond to such concerns. Again, trained celebrants spend quite a bit of time on understanding the mechanics of a funeral at a crematorium and building relationships with crematoria staff.

For many families organizing a funeral, if it has been some time since they attended one they may have few memories and expectations of what a church-led funeral can offer. They may have hazy ideas taken from family tales or from

TV dramas. One difficulty with TV funerals is that they imply that responsibility for all that happens rests with the family, so that if things go wrong the family are left to cope by themselves. For example, if a person breaks down while reading a eulogy, or a poem or Scripture, they are shown floundering at the lectern, or rushing out of the building in tears. If a fight breaks out or emotions become overwhelming in other ways the family apparently have to sort it out themselves. The minister remains seated to one side, taking no active role in anything except the formal sections of the service. In reality, the minister together with the funeral directors holds responsibility for all that happens. If someone is unable to continue with a reading, we are alert enough to step alongside and take over if needed. Helping families to know that they can trust us with the funeral and that we will ensure that everything takes place with dignity and appropriate care is important. But again, good celebrants will do this.

Offering distinctive pastoral care

For those with a Christian faith who minister to families around the time of a death, providing pastoral care and support is very important. The clergy and Readers in focus groups told many moving stories of being alongside people at a point of real need, not just to help plan a ceremony but to offer the kind of support that bears witness to God's great love for us. This kind of pastoral care is deeply valued by bereaved families, as those who talked to us both in the pilot phase and the research shared. However, having spoken to many independent celebrants, they too are motivated by compassion and care:

> *A Funeral Celebrant is a person who can help plan, write and lead a Funeral service. People from all walks of life choose to become a celebrant but all are motivated by a strong desire to help families give the person who has died a good send-off, one that honours, gives thanks for, and, even, celebrates a life.* (funeralcelebrants.org.uk)

I was speaking at an event at Sutton House, London, to promote understanding of contemporary funerals, and shared the evening with four independent celebrants, some who were deeply spiritual and some who were atheist. Each of them told the story of how they began to work as celebrants; very sadly, all the testimonies began with a personal experience of a disappointing church-led funeral. Together with a desire to make a difference to families at this crucial time, this was the motivation that drew and sustained them in their work. However, the care that celebrants can offer is necessarily limited by three important factors: time, location and community; whereas the Church has something distinctive to offer, rooted in the experience and vocation of parish ministry.

When a Church of England minister meets a bereaved family the care offered is without time or geographic limit. It is far more than one individual offering support that lasts for a few days and ends on the day of the funeral. It does not matter where a person goes or at what point in the years ahead they feel the need for support or help, the Church of England will always be there.

One vicar told me about a recently bereaved person who called one of their lay team nine months after the funeral of her partner, saying, 'I said I was okay, but really I am not. Can I still talk to you?' The answer, of course, was 'yes'. When someone calls into a church on holiday or when visiting family, and just sits quietly, or lights a candle in a cathedral, that is part of the pastoral care that the Church of England can offer.

> *'Funerals for me are really important in cathedrals too. One of the things about cathedrals is that they are always open, and so people can come, and they can light a candle, and I think that sometimes there's an anonymity about coming to a cathedral which means that people who have been bereaved will come, and come back again. And then they become part of the Church's story, of Jesus' story, and they engage with us in a way that often we don't get to see. So it's really important that we recognize that that's part of funeral ministry.'* (The Very Revd Stephen Lake, Dean of Gloucester Cathedral)

There is a wonderful story in the second book of Kings, when Elisha's attendant is terrified at the size of the army that is facing them. Elisha prays, 'O Lord, open his eyes that he may see.' And Gehazi sees that the mountains all around are filled with the army of the Lord (2 Kings 6.15–20), their confidence is renewed, and the battle is won after all. In a similar way, when a minister visits a bereaved family they do not go alone, but with the whole people of God present. Pastoral care is not just the vicar who visits: it is the coffee morning, the kind neighbour from church, the Sunday worship, the card through the door, the lunch club, joining the bellringers, and countless other activities that make up the people of God in any particular locality. The care offered by a celebrant is individual, and once the ceremony is over their involvement must of necessity come to an end.

Life Events

The Church's pastoral care is distinctive and different, offered by a faith community and not limited by time or geography, but there whenever and wherever it is needed.

Offering distinctive spiritual care

Beyond practical, emotional and pastoral care, the research showed that the Church of England has a very particular role to play in offering spiritual care to the bereaved. Across all our research around life events it has emerged that the place of prayer is valued, and that we are uniquely placed to hold spiritual conversations with people. The experience of the death of someone we know may give rise to deep questions and feelings about spiritual issues, perhaps especially a need to find comfort and hope. One of the most difficult aspects around a funeral is the gap between making the arrangements and the day of the funeral itself, which is sometimes quite lengthy:

> 'The worst part is waiting for the funeral. Definitely … You keep thinking, Oh God, how will I go on, what will I …? It's like looming ahead. It's difficult to understand. It's in your mind all the time and you're thinking, you've got to pull yourself together.'

Sometimes, particularly where the funeral is to be held at a crematorium, the delay between death and the funeral can be as much as three weeks, perhaps stretching over three weekends; this is made even more difficult if the death occurs near a major public holiday. One person talked of how the death happened in mid-December but the funeral couldn't take place until early January. The particular gift of prayer can be much appreciated at this time, as might be the space to be quiet in a church building, whether alone or as part of a worship service.

Leaving a card with the family that includes a prayer can be really helpful. The funerals team has researched and designed a card with the words, 'We don't wait till the day of the funeral to pray for you. We are praying already.' The family will know that we are there if they need us, especially if the card includes contact information. In our pilot parishes both families and ministers found it particularly helpful to leave such a card, and it often opened up conversation at a deeper level.

One vicar takes the idea further. She buys small votive candles and takes them with her to each funeral visit. At the end of the visit she offers to light the candle and say a prayer with the family. As she says, the worst that can happen is that they refuse! But mostly it is a welcome gesture. She then leaves the candle with them, so that each time they light it the prayer is echoed.

There are many stories of how the offer of prayer changes a situation. I was in a particularly difficult situation where a tragedy had affected a school. At the end of the day when all kinds of practical things had been put in place, the staff gathered together. I offered to pray. Silence fell and it was only then that tears began to fall. That is partly because of the stillness and quiet, but it is also about the presence of the Holy Spirit, which is often palpable in those kinds of circumstances. Prayer is at the heart of the distinctive spiritual care that the Church of England minister can offer to bereaved family, friends and communities. It is the way we reflect God's heart of compassion for those who mourn, simply being alongside them in their need.

Offering distinctive funerals

At the heart of a funeral visit, whether made in person or conducted over the telephone, will be the planning and preparing of the funeral ceremony or service itself. Funeral directors are likely to have outlined the structure of the service with a family at a first meeting, but this conversation may not have addressed the deeper questions about the purpose of a contemporary funeral. Families may not have much understanding about contemporary funerals, especially as expectations of funeral practice is changing rapidly. There may be real tension between the needs of a grieving family and the known or guessed wishes of the deceased, which raises a core question about the purpose of a funeral and who it is actually for.

Thanksgiving?

Overall, across the research sample, there was a clear priority for understanding the purposes of a funeral to be about thanksgiving for a life well lived, with a sense of celebration for all that the person gave to life and meant to those who remain. Underlying this is an assumption that the focus of the funeral is the person who has died, and that the service needs to reflect their contribution to the world and remember their interests and personality.

'*You know, a hymn is a hymn, But what they used to play when they were running around on their bicycles, or in their tractor, or whatever they happened to be doing, is a reminder of them, not of their surroundings, but of their life. That's important.*'

A few years ago, the TV soap *Coronation Street* featured the funeral of Hayley Cropper, who died after deciding to take her own life as she faced pancreatic cancer. Her husband Roy was vehemently opposed to this decision. Hayley planned every detail of her funeral, which was depicted in an episode shown on 31 January 2014. It was led by a celebrant and began with the Queen song 'Don't Stop Me Now', which includes the lyrics, 'Tonight, I'm gonna have myself a real good time – I feel alive'. The celebrant introduces the service as a 'celebration of life' and reminds everyone that Hayley chose the song herself because she 'thought it would make you chuckle'. There is a brightly coloured coffin, daffodils and a reading of the poem 'Do not stand at my grave and weep' (by Mary Elizabeth Frye). Throughout Roy is shown with pain etched on his face (brilliant acting!). Friends and family gather at the wake and celebrate, but Roy stands literally frozen in his anger and grief, before turning to walk out of the party, and the storyline develops as he goes missing for a few days under the weight of his grief.

This scene highlights the tension of the question around who the funeral is for – the living or the dead. In one sense it is for the living to honour the dead, but if the deceased has been able to plan ahead, it is for the deceased to identify what he or she thinks has been their contribution to life.

This emphasis on thanksgiving and celebration can lead to the sense of loss being minimized or even ignored, whereas the reality of death is often a deeply emotional experience. I was talking about this to a friend of mine – this work has meant a lot of conversations about death and funerals! My friend said, as many do, that at her funeral she wanted everyone to wear bright colours, sing happy songs and have balloons. I asked her how she felt when her own mother died – she acknowledged that it was one of the worst days of her life. So we talked about whether she had felt like 'bright colours and balloons' that day, and what it might mean to those who love her if her funeral had no place for sadness. A recent funeral visit began with a clear statement from the bereaved family that the deceased had been adamant that there was to be no grieving. But grief is a normal part of the human experience of loss and change, and balancing that with thanksgiving for good memories of the person who has died is the task of the minister and the words of the Church of England liturgy working together.

A stage of grief?

The funeral can be a clear marker on a journey of grief, marking a stage of 'letting go', and bringing some kind of closure to one part of the grief process. It is a transitional moment, perhaps moving from the initial raw pain and shock to a time when the bereaved can begin to think about some kind of future.

> A   *Closure. That's all a funeral is really.*
> B   *Closure, yeah. And you want that sense of relief that […] the church service went well.*
> A   *Once someone dies, it's awful. But once the funeral's over, you are different. You're released a bit then.*
> B   *You can still get upset all the time.*
> A   *But you let go. That's it.*

This suggests that the funeral is actually for the living, providing them with a sense of comfort, which may come from being together with others who are grieving or from the actual physical farewell to a body. But the funeral is also the final social engagement that anyone has, and the sense of accompanying the deceased to their final rest is very important. I remember the funeral of Diana, Princess of Wales, in September 1997. As the hearse went through the gates of Althorp House the commentator said, 'And that is the last we will see of Diana, Princess of Wales.' This reflects the social reality of a funeral, that transitional moment that is literally the last time we will be in the presence of the physical body of the person who has died. This is the purpose of the committal, the final moment in the service when the body is either buried or made ready for cremation; for many, the words that will resonate after the service are 'ashes to ashes, dust to dust', the timeless words that mark the ending and final farewell.

Hope for the future?

> *'[Why do we have funerals?] That's a good question. Do we do it from a spiritual point of view? Probably. Because the nearer you get to that age, the more you are likely to think, "Well, maybe there's somebody up there to help you on your way." Maybe there is, maybe there isn't. But you might as well give it a go. You've got nothing to lose.'*

Hope for the future may begin to emerge through shared memories and the presence of friends and family who offer support and comfort. A sense of hope for the living may be felt at the funeral; there is also a sense in which the Christian funeral, in particular, is about hope in a future for the deceased, although this may be somewhat tentatively expressed. This uncertainty about life after death is reflected in various ways, and is often heard in the language that people use to talk about their ideas on the subject. As I listened carefully to people's conversations at the funeral for the husband of someone who had died several years earlier, although the family had made it very clear that they were 'not religious', perhaps even atheist, there was much talk about how the deceased couple were now together again. It is not uncommon to hear families talk about people being reunited with those who have died many years earlier. It is a motif used in a wide range of stories and poems, some of which are cloyingly sentimental. Sometimes people talk about the deceased as stars or angels, or imagine them in scenarios where they would be found in their usual daily life:

> *'Just having a laugh, I said, "You'll be seeing my mum up there. You'll meet her up there and have a little drink."'*

These kinds of thoughts can easily be dismissed as 'folk religion' or 'superstition', whereas the research suggested that they may reveal hesitant thoughts about life after death. There is an opportunity for the Church to respond to these feelings, using them as a springboard to a deeper conversation, perhaps asking why that idea is important to them rather than dismissing it as trivial. This kind of conversation can be an indicator that, in spite of protestations about a lack of religious faith, a message of hope is really needed. The Christian funeral is about commending the deceased into God's care, 'in sure and certain hope of the resurrection to eternal life'. We share a message of trust in God's great mercy and love, revealed in Jesus Christ, which is hope for the deceased and hope for the living in eternity.

Above all personal?

One of the tensions that emerged from the research is the perception that the desire for a funeral to be an occasion of thanks and celebration reflecting the unique life of the deceased is in conflict with the Church's desire to share a universal message of hope.

'Generally, [funerals] all follow the same format. Just little things you can do – just like I say, the little pamphlets you can put out, different music ... And people can put a bit of thought into it and make it nice, so it connects to that one person rather than just being a basic funeral that could cover anybody really.'

It is only 40 years or so since a Church of England-led funeral would not even have included the name of the deceased, let alone anything that might be seen as personal. It is often a latent memory of this era that informs people's expectation of what a Church of England funeral might look like, and in particular their surprise that we might offer anything that could be seen as personal.

A Christian funeral can, of course, include details that are specific to an individual life, or tell the story of how that life has been lived. Psalm 139 reminds us that God has known us since we were formed in our mother's womb, and elsewhere Scripture talks of a God who knows every word we speak, is with us in all circumstances, keeps our tears in a bottle and has a plan and a purpose for our lives.

The research revealed a wide range of experiences and expectations as to whether a Church of England-led funeral could or would be personal. A contrast is often drawn between our expectations of a church-led funeral and that led by someone else:

'No disrespect to priests, but they're brought up on their religious learning. They've got a format. He might talk a bit religious; then he might say a few prayers; then he might in general say a few things [about the person], but not a lot. And then you'd have some hymns ... A humanist talks about everything. It covers a person's life ... If priests could do that, they could also keep the religious bit if they wanted to.'

The word 'humanist' is not necessarily being used to describe the faith position of a Humanist, but perhaps might better be understood as someone 'humanly warm', or personal, reflecting an interest and concern for the deceased and the family who are at the heart of the service. Sometimes it takes families by surprise when they experience a level of personal concern from church ministers: 'The vicar was nice. He took quite a bit of time and got to know us.'

Creating a funeral ceremony that is perceived as personal is not just about the way in which the minister or celebrant relates to the family, and takes time to hear the story of the life of the deceased. Choices can be made that may help a funeral to feel personal – flowers, types of coffin, location, venue. Sometimes people need to be reassured that having a church or church-led funeral does not mean that they are restricted in their choice of coffin, for example – there is nothing to say they can't have a willow coffin or a cardboard coffin or even one that looks like a phone box. Other choices open to the family include the placing of mementoes or photographs. I took a funeral at a crematorium where the deceased was a huge sports fan, including Gloucester rugby. After talking with the family about their needs and expectations, rather than robes I wore a clerical shirt and dog collar with a red jacket and skirt (the team's colours). Although such choices help to make a funeral feel distinctive, three elements in particular stand out as crucial in making the occasion personal, and these are areas where families may have real anxiety about what the church will 'allow'. These three elements are music, readings, and the eulogy or tribute. The importance of each of these, and how they contribute to making a service seem personal, is explored below.

Popular music – the poetry of our time

Music can be a contentious issue at funerals, but it is likely to become increasingly important as we come alongside the 'baby boomers' and subsequent generations in the next few decades. This generation has been shaped by popular music in a way that is different from previous generations; people now develop personal playlists that help them to tell the story of their lives. Whether it is *Desert Island Discs* or 'Inheritance Tracks' on *Saturday Live* with the Revd Richard Coles (both on Radio 4) or 'Tracks of my Years' on Radio 2, music tells stories. For many people, these choices of music will be drawn from a wide range of genres, and may or may not include classical or sacred music – although I have met families selecting choral recordings of 'The Lord's my Shepherd' and the Lord's Prayer as sung by the Italian tenor Andrea Bocelli, rather than hymns.

> *Not only has music been associated with death and grief, whether in the laments of many traditional societies or in the worldwide culture of requiem masses, but it has found a welcome home in Western societies as an expression of grief that fits with many musical genres.* (Douglas Davies, *Mors Britannica*, p. 189)

There is a wonderful scene from the TV comedy *Car Share* (BBC 1, Episode 1, Series 2, April 2015) where the two central characters are travelling to a colleague's funeral, which leads to a discussion about 'what song you'll have at your funeral'. It is both extremely funny and also poignant and insightful. It highlights that song lyrics have become the new poetry – many people no longer have a memory bank of well-known poetry to draw on to help express deep feelings. Instead the lyrics of a song may put into words people's thoughts and emotions that would otherwise remain unsaid (although reading the lyrics of S Club 7's 'Reach' may be a little unusual!). The episode reflects a mixture of traditional and contemporary expectations of all that a funeral might involve – and is well worth a view.

Fear about whether 'the Church' will allow their choice of music is one of the reasons why a family might opt for a funeral led by a celebrant. The Church has a reputation for making judgements on popular culture, whereas a family's choice of a song is about their story and their memories rather than ours. It may be that we need to offer practical advice about music – sometimes people only know the chorus or a couple of a lines from a song, and checking out the whole lyric means a new level of meaning is revealed. The emotional intensity of listening to a song at the crematorium or in the church may be quite different from being able to weep quietly as you do the ironing. The significance of a song may be changed for ever once it has been connected to a funeral. I was driving to visit my family on Christmas Day, more than a decade after my mum's funeral, when 'Morning Town Ride' by the Seekers came on the radio. For me, that is forever linked with her funeral, and I thought I might have to stop driving as the memories came back.

Some of the most moving and emotional moments at funerals happen around music. I happened to take a funeral where Johnny Logan, twice Eurovision Song Contest winner, sang in person 'Waltzing Matilda' in honour of an Australian friend, and it turned out to be a beautiful lament. Another time a heavy metal band were due to perform but realized that their equipment would blow up the church's primitive sound system, so two members did an acoustic version of 'My Guitar Gently Weeps' to honour their roadie friend. After the service everyone swept off to the cemetery on motor bikes, including the curate (but not the vicar!). As the baby boom generation plans and organizes funerals, so music will become increasingly important, not only in reflecting the significant moments in a life that has been lived, but also in expressing the emotions that people feel. At the same time, knowledge of hymns is decreasing. Families can listen to a selection of funeral hymns on the Church of England website (www. churchofenglandfunerals.org), but it may be helpful also to suggest recorded versions, especially if the service is at a crematorium. It can be important to 'give permission' not to include a hymn, if a family is really not comfortable, especially at a service in a location other than a church building. When families do suggest hymns, they may not be those we are expecting; it is important that we listen to the reasons for people's choices, being sensitive in our responses and advice.

'I said, "We're gonna have the same [hymns] as when we got married." And she [the vicar] said, "Oh, you don't want them." And I said, "I want the same ones as when we got married." I insisted that I had "Love Divine" and "The Lord is My Shepherd". In the end she was a bit narky.'

Readings

Readings are an area of further choice for families putting a funeral service together. A Church of England-led funeral must include a reading from the Bible, and should include a psalm or a hymn (see notes to the funeral service, *Common Worship: Pastoral Services*, p. 291). As with hymns, families with little or no formal church connections may have few ideas about Bible readings, and the minister may want to share some options with them to help them make a choice. In addition, many families want to include other readings that seem to express their feelings and thoughts. Some of these have become well known having featured in films or on television or been widely used on greetings cards. One of these is the famous 'Death is nothing at all' passage taken from Henry Scott Holland's sermon in 1910 while King Edward VII was lying in state.

Its popular familiarity carries with it a kind of secular religious tone that is not, however, devoid of resonance with traditional Christian affirmation of the on-going identity of the dead 'in another place'. (Douglas Davies, *Mors Britannica*, p. 159)

A similar sentiment, which seems like a denial of the reality of grief and death, is found in the popular poem 'Do not stand at my grave and weep' by Mary Elizabeth Frye. These words express something of the complexity of emotions around death, including the sense that a person is very much still in our thoughts and memories, together with the hope that death is not the end of a relationship. I remember discovering that those I loved deeply were more present to me in their absence than they had ever been in their lifetime as they occupied my thoughts in the initial months of grief. I wrote a great deal about absence and presence and the relationship between that and the hope of eternity. Those we meet who are grieving may find the words of popular culture give voice to some of these thoughts. Readings chosen by the family may allow the minister who speaks an opportunity to make connections with the good news of God's love in Jesus Christ and the message of hope alongside the reality of human imaginings and metaphors. There can be something surprising when we realize the universality of feelings of grief across time and cultures, linking together words from our current century with the poetry of the psalms or the letters of St Paul from two or three thousand years earlier. Love and grief have always been part of our human experience, and have always found a place in the reflections and prayers of those who seek to make sense of life and death.

Telling their story – the eulogy

The choice or importance of music and readings may well help to shape the personal nature of the funeral, and may also provide a link to what has become a central part of the contemporary funeral – the eulogy. This is an opportunity for the life of the person who has died to be reviewed and how this is done is part of what makes the funeral personal. For a celebrant this is at the core of the service – a great deal of time will be spent in listening carefully and crafting well. Some training courses for celebrants include in the admissions criteria evidence of an ability to write well. Good practice involves sending the eulogy to the family beforehand and giving them a copy afterwards, regardless of who delivers the speech on the day.

Our research with bereaved families found that contributing to the funeral is an important part of the bereavement process for many people, and for some that means being able to deliver the eulogy themselves. Increasingly, dramatized funerals on TV show family members speaking a tribute or reading a poem, which has led to the growing expectation that this happens at every funeral.

At one level this is as simple as being able to do something for the person who has died:

> *'To me it's a way of remembering the person, and feeling that you're doing the last thing that you can for them.'*

One family, who had lost an adult daughter, talked movingly of never being able to do anything for her again as we shaped a fairly elaborate funeral service. I myself remember wanting to say something at my father's funeral, along with my sister, feeling that I should be able to do for him something I spend my days doing for others.

But families often need help in crafting a eulogy. This may be the first time they have planned a funeral, or spoken in public, and practical advice and encouragement are much appreciated. At a very basic level, it may be helping them to know that 100 words takes around a minute to deliver – and that one side of A4 typed is usually around 500 words. That can be particularly relevant when time is very limited at a crematorium. Or it can be that they need some guidance as to how to tell the story of a life, rather than just memories from one perspective.

> *'The curate came to my house and discussed the funeral arrangements with myself and my daughters. She wasn't forceful, just gave some ideas which we were receptive to, and generally speaking helped us to understand the service, what she thought was appropriate. This was a great help and comfort to us.'*

Considerate celebrants who sensitively respond to the explicit or implicit need to participate are spoken of in glowing terms. This could be in the form of encouragement, advice or suggestions about the ceremony (some even provided informal coaching to the bereaved). Even if it is simply expressing the option that they can change their minds about how much to be involved, this is experienced by families as being included in the funeral service on the day. For ministers, a service held in the local church may well give more scope to help a family play a part, for example by offering space to rehearse or visit beforehand to check the detail and the choreography of the day.

> *'The vicar didn't have much to do with it because my daughter's done it. We had him on standby in case she couldn't do it, but she did. He said, "Go on down to the church and practise if you want; do whatever you want." So that's what happened. They went down there a few times, the girls [to practise the eulogy].'*

This expresses really well the relationship between the bereaved and the minister as 'co-creators' or at least co-participants in the funeral service. Although the respondent perceives that the vicar's role was minimal, in reality the vicar had done a huge amount by providing the space and supporting the family through the process. In his book *Meaningful Funerals*, Ewan Kelly writes of the importance of the relationship between the minister and the bereaved in listening and learning from one another. However, he notes that the relationship is never one of equals: the minister shares experience and knowledge and information to help the family shape a funeral that is relevant to their loved one and their needs. Kelly also notes:

> *The bereaved are not looking for answers from a church representative in their acute grief but an opportunity to give vent to what is a deep and heartfelt desire to try to make sense of what has happened and why.* (p. 136)

The Church of England funeral liturgy

At the heart of a Christian funeral the story of a life that has been lived will be held within the story of God's great love for humankind revealed in Jesus Christ. The message of hope that is rooted in the Christian gospel will permeate funerals that are led by a Christian minister from the opening words. If a funeral is held in church, then the very building itself is bearing witness to the faithfulness of God and the enduring message of Jesus. Recently I conducted a funeral in a rural village where there had been a church since 687 – 1,300 years of faithful witness. There was something very special about saying the words of the Lord's Prayer and knowing that they had been said in that place for generation after generation.

Our research began to explore the experience and expectations of the bereaved about the importance of the Christian message and also how it might best be shared at a time of loss, not just in a sermon but throughout the service, in the words of the funeral liturgy itself. In the midst of the emotional intensity of grief it is unlikely that people will remember any details of what was said, particularly if it is seen as being simply routine rather than relevant to them.

> *The research highlighted that a certain amount of the liturgy read out in a* **typical funeral service is absorbed more as 'background noise'** *rather than fully comprehended and absorbed, owing perhaps to the speed of delivery and its generic feel: 'this is the bit they always say, I don't need to listen yet'. For some, these elements of the service risk being irrelevant, strange or alienating.* (ESRO research report)

As already noted, celebrants should give families a printed copy of all that has been said at the service, so they can read it again later. Many people will keep 'memory boxes', storing cards, service sheets, letters and other things that were meaningful at the time of the funeral. It may be worth considering doing something along these lines; respondents suggested that there is a need for something familiar and comforting that expresses hope in something that goes beyond the limitations of our human experience. There is a sense that the words of the liturgy, in particular the commendation and committal, express something really important. But at the same time there is a need for those words to be said with warmth and engagement rather than simply as a matter of course.

> *'[Priests] are lovely people and their religion is nice. I think they've got to lighten up a bit. Maybe if a priest went and sat down and listened to a service by a humanist, I'm sure they'd think to themselves, "There's something there we could do."'*

Insight into these expectations came when I was attending a seminar at the Ideal Death Show. This experience was described in Part Two on baptism, but is important enough to be worth repeating here. A leading trainer on public speaking described two modes of addressing an audience: what she calls 'cat' and 'dog' mode.

'Dog mode' is when a speaker is warm, friendly and engaging, reaching out to the audience and wanting to be with them. 'Cat mode' is when a speaker is formal and distant, only inviting the audience into relationship on their terms. Both modes need to be used, in combination. What was significant was that after describing 'cat mode', she added, 'like vicars'. The expectation is that we are only ever in formal mode – so when we step out of that and become warm and engaging, the response is one of surprise and delight. If, standing outside the church after conducting a funeral, we are greeted with the words, 'That was the best funeral I have ever attended,' we might think it a somewhat surprising reaction! Balancing 'dog' and 'cat' modes is the key to being warm and personal at funerals. There is a right moment to be formal, particularly around the commendation and committal, but also many moments to move towards people with smiles and kindness.

The shape of the funeral service

There are many books offering ideas and resources for use at a funeral, and the liturgical framework is one of the most flexible. It is worth noting how often the phrase 'in these or other words' appears, and that tiny word 'may', so easily overlooked, is surprisingly common in the funeral liturgy.

The basic shape of the service, wherever a minister is leading it, is very simple:

- **The gathering** – This is about creating a sense of community for the occasion, welcome, and telling people what is going to happen. The minister may greet the coffin at the door or accompany it into the space, and may decide to read some of the suggested sentences at this point. The contemporary *Common Worship* service also includes the possibility of penitence, which can be an important space for people to acknowledge painful feelings and difficult memories, but it will need to be sensitive to the circumstances.
- **Readings and sermons** – There may be more than one reading, including some that are secular. There must be one reading from the Bible, which should be from the New Testament, and after the reading will be a good time to use a hymn or a psalm – singing or listening to 'The Lord is my Shepherd' might be particularly appropriate. The *Common Worship* structure suggests that a tribute is given earlier and separately from readings and a sermon. In practice, particularly where time is short at a crematorium, green burial site

or funeral director's chapel, and where the minister has been trusted to do all the speaking, these may merge together. There is further reflection on preaching at funerals later in this section.

- **Prayers** – Although there is a suggested sequence in *Common Worship*, this may be an opportunity to be both reflective and personal. If the funeral congregation is familiar with responses, then it may be helpful to use them, but for most, simply saying 'Amen' will be sufficient. The Lord's Prayer is not compulsory, but for many these will be the most familiar words in the service, bearing a weight of meaning and memory. The traditional language version is still likely to be the one that is stored deep in people's memory, although this may depend on local practice.
- **Commendation, farewell and committal** – The simple formality of the words that are said marks the most important part of the service, as the deceased is commended to God, and a final farewell is said. Some ministers like to touch the coffin, but it is worth asking the family if that is acceptable – some may feel that it is an invasion of privacy, and I recently met someone who reacted very badly to seeing it happen. The words for committal are arguably the most beautiful in the service, the kind of traditional phrases that are 'hallowed by use'. Although people may not remember the words in detail, they will convey compassion, significance and hope. The service then ends with a final prayer for those gathered.

This shape works really well if the service is to take place in one location, or within a fairly narrow time-frame. A church funeral service followed by a burial in the surrounding churchyard has a timeless beauty that I always find incredibly moving. The service also works well at the crematorium, although some sections will need to be conflated, especially as many crematoria have very stringent – and frustrating – time limits. It can be much more difficult if there is a long gap between the end of a church service and the final committal, perhaps where the crematorium is several miles away and may take an hour to get to. It may be worth talking to the family about other possibilities. I led a funeral recently where the committal happened at the lychgate: friends poured out of church, gathered round, and the final words were said as the coffin was placed in the hearse. The guests and wider family were able to remain together and go to the wake; I travelled with the coffin and a few close family members to the crematorium, said a short prayer with them and then returned to join the rest of the guests. This needs to be discussed carefully and thoughtfully with the family, but may work well in some situations.

There is an emerging trend for requesting cremation before the funeral service, which can be challenging. This choice may be for practical reasons – it is a lot easier to get a slot at a crematorium either early or late in the day, for example. However, they may not be good times for guests to gather. It may also collude with a cultural tendency to deny the reality of death, and it is difficult, if not impossible, to have a funeral service without a body. The service that follows the cremation is closer to a memorial service, which offers a flexible framework but may miss the sense of saying farewell to a person. It resonates with the earlier questions and thoughts about the purpose of a funeral, and who it is actually for and about.

Here's one story of an 'ordinary' funeral:

'The trouble with being a clergyman is that when one's asked about remembering funerals you remember the slightly unusual ones, shall we say? I remember one, I was … I saw this bloke in hospital and he was very near the end of his life. He was asleep and I sat down by the bed and I was praying quietly for a moment. He opened his eyes – I won't say the exact words that he used but it was words to the effect of "What are you doing here?" So we had a conversation and four days later the hospital rang up and said he'd died and one of the last things he said was, was that bleepity bleep bleep bleep vicar willing to do the funeral? [laughs] So, anyhow, the funeral party started well before the funeral, in the local pub, which he had propped up the bar of for many years – he had no family living. And it was his friends at the pub who carried him into the funeral and into the church. And it turned into a dialogue. So every time I asked a rhetorical question, they all shouted out the answers. [broad smile] Now, that is not a typical funeral in one sense, though, actually, it led to all kinds of good things because, what it was, was that I worked very hard to make them feel that they were valued; that they were part of the process. That they were saying goodbye in an important way. And I also said something about Jesus. And they listened. Briefly. [laughs] And I think what was good about that was not that it was, you know, a typical funeral – whatever that may be because every individual is different; so, typical is a difficult word – but, it was about the focus on the individual and the focus on the mourners. And I think that is what the Church of England does well.' (Archbishop Justin Welby)

The Church of England's *Common Worship: Pastoral Services* has a wealth of material that can be used in a whole range of circumstances; by varying prayers, readings and sentences, the service can become very personal to the family and their circumstances. Many of us spend a long time crafting services when a death has occurred through a tragedy or is untimely. I have seen so many beautiful liturgies for stillborn babies, put together with care and compassion to meet the deepest of needs. I have attended sensitive services for a person who took their own life or had their life taken from them violently, and I know that we spend huge amounts of time around these events. However, the majority of funerals that we take will be for those who die in the fullness of years, aged 75 and over, and being able to reflect through the service that each life mattered and each person is loved by God helps to build the relationship with the bereaved. The good news that emerged from the research is that many church-led funerals are meeting family needs by offering a warm, personal and hopeful funeral service. As part of the research process, many funerals were observed in both church and crematoria. One of the independent researchers noted:

> *'What struck me the most, I think, was how varied the funerals were, in terms of how much effort the celebrant was making to make the funerals personal and unique. The best celebrants, including some Church of England celebrants, were really quite breathtaking. The services were at once moving, memorable, poignant, very sensitive, and in many cases quite beautiful.'*

Preaching at funerals

Ministers have a responsibility to preach at a funeral service. This might be a separate address set apart from a eulogy, or, particularly when time is tight, it may link the story of the deceased with the sharing of Christian hope. The research revealed that what is important to the bereaved is that any address is relevant and accessible, grounded in the needs and circumstances of the family, and that it has an integrity that reflects both the love and mercy of God in Christ and the current reality of the mourners' spiritual understanding – given that that will vary widely. It is part of the reality of sharing the gospel that we can acknowledge loss and yet talk about thanksgiving and delight in the life that has been lived.

To focus only on our lament and loss during a funeral without thanksgiving or celebration is to deny the significance of the deceased's life to mourners in the past, present and future and our belief, as church representatives, in resurrection. (Ewan Kelly, *Meaningful Funerals*, p. 140)

The sermons that make the most impression on mourners are those that are delivered with genuine warmth and interest, reflecting humour and compassion, and above all feeling personal. Although the minister may never have met the deceased, or known anything of the family until meeting them, he or she can convey a sense of common humanity, reflecting something of the John Donne poem, 'No Man is an Island':

Any man's death diminishes me,
Because I am involved in mankind,
And therefore never send to know for whom the bell tolls;
It tolls for thee.

The recognition that this is a unique life that has ended, and that the loss of that life will make a difference to those gathered, enables people to begin to hear something of the hope that is offered in a Church of England-led funeral. The compassion and kindness shown by the minister is a reflection of the compassion and kindness that God shows to those who are bereaved, and the message of love and mercy in Jesus that opens up hope grows out of that warmth.

Sometimes examples of good preaching at funerals become well known. In April 2017, the Very Revd Andrew Nunn, Dean of Southwark, preached at the funeral of PC Keith Palmer, killed in a terrorist attack in Westminster. Andrew drew on images of Keith's life and the fact that he died sacrificially, and linked them movingly to the Gospel reading and the story of Easter. The sermon made a big impact, with comments in newspapers and on social media as people not only heard the comfort offered to the family and the gratitude for a life well lived, but also heard the heart of the gospel message again, that love will triumph over hatred and death.

In a different context, the Revd Juliet Stephenson, the Good Funeral Awards Funeral Celebrant of the Year 2015, talks of how being part of the community helps her to shape funeral addresses:

Life Events

'If someone dies in my community, chances are I will know them and chances are that I've baptized a few children in that family. I may also know some of the children within that family group because I go to primary schools, speak at assemblies and do after-school activities.'

The Revd Giles Fraser recently spoke at the funeral of a friend of mine, a committed Christian who died suddenly aged 51. He talked with warmth of her involvement in the life of the church, he made us laugh, he helped us remember. He talked of her faith, and then he began to tell a particular story of how she was present at the Easter Vigil earlier in the year. He recalled her voice singing in the darkness in response to the words, 'The Light of Christ'. Then he took the Paschal candle from its stand just in front of the coffin. He walked to the back of the church, then moved forward, singing the same Easter words, and we all responded, 'Thanks be to God.' It was a powerful verbal and visual proclamation of hope, and a deeply personal and memorable sermon, the kind of funeral that makes a difference, the kind that ministers are leading throughout the country.

There is no doubt that the expectations and experience of a contemporary twenty-first-century funeral are changing and will continue to do so. Good secular celebrants are working in a way that engages the family, enables them to feel part of the process and reflects their needs so that they feel emotionally supported. One of the challenges facing the Church of England is how to resource the level of engagement that this takes. Celebrants who are spending 10–14 hours preparing a funeral may be working solely on funeral ministry, whereas a church minister is having to invest in a whole range of other issues and situations. Some dioceses are beginning to explore possibilities such as training individuals who feel particularly called to ministry around death, dying and funerals, and freeing them from other responsibilities. But alongside the resource demand, there is the very real difficulty of a lack of knowledge among both the public and funeral directors as to just what a contemporary funeral led by a Church of England minister might actually offer. And that's the third key insight that will be considered.

3 The Church needs to communicate clearly what we offer

As part of the research background we conducted an Omnibus survey (a broad-based quantitative survey which assesses attitudes, behaviours and opinions) to discover whether people actually know what they can ask for in a Church of England-led funeral. As all clergy know, everyone within a parish is entitled to a Church of England-led funeral service, but nationally fewer than half the population are aware of this. As knowledge of what the Church does and what it offers diminishes generation after generation, it has become more important that we make sure that people have good practical guidance as to what might be available.

The in-depth research revealed a great deal of confusion, especially about the language of 'church' and what might be possible. Some research respondents thought that those who attend church would have preferential treatment, while others thought that to have a burial you have to have a church funeral:

'I really want to be buried. That, by definition – unless you tell me otherwise – means I have to have some sort of church funeral.'

This confusion is exacerbated around cremation, with real uncertainty about the role of the Church:

'We didn't have a church service because she didn't want one. But we did have the local vicar come to the crematorium and talk about her.'

Such misunderstandings about the Church's role in funerals can lead to wishes being ignored, or not fulfilled. Someone may be asked if they want a church funeral, but they may decline because they wish to be cremated, yet a Church of England minister can lead a funeral at a crematorium or cemetery chapel, or at a chapel on a funeral director's premises.

The confusion goes further if people have strong views about whether a church is a good place to have a funeral, if church is associated with awkward access and limited facilities, for example, and perhaps little choice about the type of music or other options that might be available. On the other hand,

147

some find church as a fitting place at the heart of the community, something particularly strong in rural areas. It is notable that the highest proportion of church-led funerals per head of the population occurs in rural dioceses, such as Carlisle and Hereford. Others find the idea of crematoria off-putting, with memories of places that are impersonal or functional, being described as 'stark' or 'unfriendly'. However, in the current context over 70 per cent of all funerals will involve cremation, so it is important that people know that the church is involved here as well.

One of the commonest words to emerge from the research is 'allowed'. People are not sure what we do as a Church, where funerals can happen and who is eligible. They worry that their choices will not be 'allowed' in church, or about whether their local vicar will be 'allowed' to conduct a ceremony at the crematorium.

Much confusion was evident around woodland burial grounds. Woodland burial grounds have increased rapidly in number over the past decade; there are now over 270 such sites in England, and not all are registered with the Association of National Burial Grounds. There is a great variety, ranging from small privately owned sites to those owned by large corporate companies; others are operated by local authorities alongside more traditional sites. The research suggested that woodland burial sites are spoken of as a 'perfect way to go', but there was uncertainty about the Church's willingness to be at such ceremonies. It is difficult to find information about whether a church minister can be involved with a woodland burial – searching for information will lead to sites such as the Natural Death Centre, which only talks about celebrants, inadvertently implying that religious ministers may not be permitted or willing to be involved. However, the Diocese of Ely runs its own natural burial ground, Barton Glebe, which was the focus of one of the most extensive pieces of research carried out concerning woodland burial (see Douglas Davies and Hannah Rumble, *Natural Burial*).

What natural burial sites do offer is a degree of openness for the imagination, whether for the living anticipating their own grave site or bereaved people thinking about their dead kin … In all of this the imagination plays with death and allows a relative to speak of how a dead person would be happy in a spot where he can 'see things' in a particular direction, or where she may anticipate birdsong. Even notions of time – itself a deeply embedded cultural category –

are affected by natural burial sites, where, for example, the notion of eternity that was pervasive in traditional churchyards and cemeteries through formal texts on headstones is replaced by the environmental signs of the seasons and the settling of the grave. (Douglas Davies, *Mors Britannica*, p. 361)

There is no reason why a Church of England minister should not lead a service for a woodland burial in an authorized burial ground, but among both clergy and people there is confusion as to what might actually be possible. As this type of burial is set to become more popular in the decades ahead, it may well be important to enure that people know that this is a possibility. It also highlights the importance of funeral directors having accurate information to give out about what local Church of England ministers are able to offer.

During the pilot phase of the research, with 150 parishes across four dioceses, we tested a number of tools that would enable churches to communicate clearly what a Church of England-led funeral might involve to both funeral directors and the public. We produced a simple leaflet for distribution in any place where people are looking for information about funeral options, such as libraries, Age UK offices, funeral directors and crematoria (the leaflet is available from www. churchprinthub.org).

I saw a Facebook post recently that featured a crematorium noticeboard with information about around 50 celebrants on display but nothing at all about the Church of England, Christian ministers or other faith-based options. My local crematorium has a publicity stand with lots of useful leaflets, but again, nothing from the Church.

The Church of England's national website (churchofenglandfunerals.org) has lots of clear information and help about all that is available. This is rapidly becoming one of the first sites families find when they begin to look for information online. There is a simple 'business card' available which features the web address, making it ideal to leave in places where people pick up information (also available from www.churchprinthub.org). As a result of the pilot phase, our resources and wording were developed and changed, but the impact and usefulness of the information is clearly valued.

One funeral director spoke to a local clergy person about the leaflet we produced:

'I didn't know this, I didn't know that, and I really love this leaflet so that I can show that to people when they come in, because that's just reminded me of the breadth of welcome, of the hospitality that you give people. You don't have to come to church – you're there for everybody.'

Another simple tool is a bookmark, which invites those attending a funeral to pray for the family afterwards and draws them to the website where they can light an online candle as a sign of prayer (available from www.churchprint hub.org). This bookmark can be overprinted with the contact details of a local church or minister, and is particularly helpful at crematoria services, where people can leave afterwards with no clear idea of who was involved in leading the service and helping the family. However, we discovered that if the bookmarks are simply left in the pews/seats, they will still be there at the end of the service. If the minister talks about praying for the family after the day, and then hands the bookmarks to people at the door, they get taken away. In fact, on a number of occasions people have asked for more than one – for example, when the deceased had been resident in a nursing home and their friends had been unable to travel to the funeral, the bookmarks were taken back to give to other residents.

Communicating confidence

A key message that we have identified across all our research is that the Church of England needs to be more confident in letting people know what it can offer at life's key moments. Although funeral services can generate strong reactions, and for some lead to a negative experience and low expectations, there is still a strong appreciation that a Church of England-led funeral meets real needs, and the efforts made to help and advise families are much appreciated. The Church of England funeral is deeply personal, full of comfort, allows flexibility to reflect personal choices, and yet has a timelessness that brings peace and, above all, hope. Yet people do not always know that this is on offer, and information on websites and in printed leaflets from other organizations is not necessarily accurate, so making sure that local funeral directors, libraries, community and commercial websites have good information is important.

'He was nice when he came to the house. He got to know quite a bit and he spoke to quite a few of us. I think the vicar was what held it together, more than the funeral director, with the technical things – "Do this, do that, cost this" – tell you what you need to know. But the vicar was more homely, more friendly.'

Over and again our researchers noted that while the Church of England is not doing anything that actually pushes people away, it is doing little to pull people towards us. It requires a shift of thinking to realize that we now have to tell people who we are and what we do, rather than assuming they know. And there is one particular group of people with whom we need to communicate effectively if we are to be involved in funeral ministry for the long term. The next key insight emerging from the research highlights the relationship between the local church and the funeral director.

4 Building professional partnerships is essential

'The relationship with funeral directors is, for me, one of the key elements of funeral ministry. I've had the privilege of working with some very good funeral directors. And the result of that was seeing the huge contribution they make to what is always an agonizing process for a family – in terms of the family feeling that they can get through this. It's an amazing partnership when it can be made to work. But the relationship does depend on good communication. And so it needs to be personal and it needs to be professional.' (Archbishop Justin Welby)

At the heart of all our research findings there is an emphasis on building relationship, with couples, parents and families. In funeral ministry, that relationship is built and sustained from first contact with a bereaved person, continues through the leading of the service and then has the potential to go into the future. In and through all of that we reflect the relationship that God has through Jesus Christ with each one of us and pray that those we meet will discover something of the love, life and community that is available.

But the Church of England's ministry around death and funerals is significantly different from our ministry around marriage and baptism of a child. In the hours or days following a death, the family will contact a funeral director – and the funeral director is the key to organizing the care of the body and the ritual that will mark this death. We need to build relationships with funeral directors.

Although there are still circumstances where the minister may be contacted very soon after a death – or may even have been present – these are increasingly rare. Even if someone does call us personally to talk about a death with a clear expectation that there will be church-led and perhaps a church-located funeral service, the details will be arranged through the funeral director.

Our researchers discovered that the role of the funeral director is highly valued by those organizing funerals:

> 'They take a lot of the burden off you. Because they straight away move in, and you're in shock, and then they go through everything that needs doing. So you've got to get a good funeral director. And it takes all the responsibility off you.'

It is difficult to get an accurate figure of the number of funeral directors in England as it is an unregulated industry, but for the United Kingdom as a whole, it is estimated that there are around 4,000 businesses, ranging from large corporate enterprises to family-run concerns. The industry is said to be worth around a billion pounds annually, with 25 per cent of business being accounted for by two major companies, the Co-operative Group and Dignity Caring Funerals. The Co-operative Group (CWS Ltd) has over 675 branches across the United Kingdom, and Dignity has around 500 branches (www.uk-funerals.co.uk).

There are three major trade organizations for funeral directors:

- The National Association of Funeral Directors (NAFD)
- Society of Allied and Independent Funeral Directors (SAIF)
- The National Federation of Funeral Directors (NFFD).

Each of these organizations works to promote excellence in the funeral industry, offering training and support and promoting good practice. They will work together on issues that affect the industry, for example, encouraging members to sign up to fair pricing policies and campaigning around funeral poverty. Traditionally known as undertakers, contemporary businesses are nearly always known as 'funeral directors' and that is the industry's preferred title for this sphere of work.

The role of a funeral director is a broad service encompassing practical organization, support and guidance to the family and liaison with a wide range of other organizations to ensure the funeral is properly arranged. (NAFD website)

The breadth of the funeral world

Nowhere is the range and depth of funeral directors' concerns more evident than at the biennial National Funeral Exhibition. Although not the only trade show for the funeral industry, nor the only opportunity for professionals to gather, it is a most important date in the calendar for all who are involved. I first discovered this event in June 2013 and one of the most surprising things about it was the very low-key involvement of churches. Churches Together have always had a small stand, for little or no cost, staffed by one or two ministers from different denominations, including Quakers, Methodists and Church of England representatives. However, given that the Church of England is still involved in over a third of all deaths nationally, here was an opportunity to use the exhibition to communicate within the industry as fellow professionals. The show includes hearses and horses, lots of coffins, technical support, burial grounds, stonemasons, printers, florists and much more. In subsequent exhibitions, in 2015 and 2017, the Church of England has had a very large stand, which attracted a good deal of positive comment from other professionals and funeral directors, many of them delighted to see us there. In addition, as part of our first national conference on funeral ministry we took almost 200 delegates to spend a morning at the exhibition, and that visit made a huge impact on exhibitors, visitors and delegates alike.

For the exhibitors, it was quite a shock to find so many clergy and ministers attending the exhibition, but once they began to talk to each other, the benefits began to emerge. Mutual respect flourished and fresh understanding developed around what is involved in all the different aspects of caring for others at the time of a funeral. Funeral directors and their staff who were visiting the exhibition also really appreciated meeting church ministers:

'*It was a pleasure to see you all at the NFE. We need to see more of the church.*'

For the church ministers the visit was sometimes eye-opening, as they talked to those whose work is often unseen, meeting skilled professionals who make coffins or care for bodies. There was some surprise at the range of bereavement charities present, and church ministers began to realize that the Church is not the only group interested in offering support after the funeral. New technologies and new ways of remembering loved ones were also noticed, and delegates came away with a new awareness of the funeral world:

> *'I left the exhibition knowing (and I am almost ashamed to admit it) that my presence is just one moment within a process of death, dying and bereavement that extends well beyond my best efforts in ways I hadn't previously thought about.'* (Clergy delegate at NFE, 2015)

The role of the funeral director

Given the key role that funeral directors play in supporting families after a death, we have done several pieces of research within the industry and conducted conversations with leading members of the professional bodies as well as CEOs of the larger groups. Alongside this our research with bereaved families shaped our understanding about the role of the funeral director and the importance of the relationships between family, minister and the funeral director's business. The funeral director is seen as someone who gives advice to a family, and that advice is trusted and followed.

> *'They understand what you're going through. They understand you really. They don't say, "We'll do this £7,000 one." They go through what you think, they let you choose. They don't, although you do choose, they don't recommend that. They say, "Depending on how much you want to spend", and they show you different ones. And you take your time. That was good. I wasn't rushed or told what you … you should have that. Nothing like that.'*

This has significant implications for the Church of England. It is the funeral director, or their staff, who negotiates the choice of 'celebrant' for the funeral service itself. If a family have clearly identified who they want, then the funeral director will always honour those wishes, but very few people have actually made those wishes known or written them down. However, as funeral directors increasingly promote pre-paid funeral plans, such wishes will be put in place. Many of these plans make no reference to the possibility of a minister of religion or a place of worship being used for the service. If the family haven't identified the celebrant, the next question is usually framed along the lines of, 'Were they religious?' Again, if the family give a clear answer, identifying a specific faith, churchgoing or atheism, then the funeral director will follow their lead. But the question can be a difficult one to answer. First, being 'religious' is not always seen as a positive attribute, and may readily be pushed aside. Or it may be that an older relative dies after some years in a care home and all memory of past faith or knowledge of regular attendance at monthly services in the home has disappeared. So people may answer uncertainly. The funeral director might then suggest the local vicar, if they have a relationship with them. If that vicar is responsive and available, then they may choose the suggested vicar. Otherwise, the funeral director will turn to an independent or civil celebrant.

During the pilot phase of this work some of those who took part began to explore with local funeral directors how this question might be framed differently. For example, instead of asking whether the deceased was religious, the question might be whether they would like a hymn and a prayer in the funeral service. This may be a better indicator of the family's need and openness to spiritual content. Increasingly, large funeral director businesses will employ a 'funeral arranger', the person responsible for meeting clients and sorting all the details of the service. Often these people may have limited knowledge and experience of church-led funerals, particularly as they do not usually attend the funeral service itself. This means that there can be opportunities for us to offer help and information so that families can be given the best service possible. The families trust the advice of the funeral director and will usually accept their recommendation as to the most appropriate celebrant for their situation:

'Because it feels safe, I'd go with whoever is appointed me for the day.'

It is interesting to note when in conversation with funeral directors how quickly they begin to tell stories of church ministers who have been difficult or awkward, and proceed to say what is wrong with the Church of England's approach to funeral ministry. Unsurprisingly, when we talked in focus groups with clergy and Readers, they had tales of difficult funeral directors and spoke of why it was challenging to work with them. In reality, there are very good funeral directors – just as there are very good ministers – and some that are disappointing. But the vast majority are motivated by serving the needs of families, because their reputation, longevity and business success is based on providing an exceptional service at one of the most difficult times in anyone's life. Two key factors emerged from our research with funeral directors about what they want from a celebrant:

- They look for someone who will meet the needs of the family.
- They want someone who is easy to work with, which means available and customer-focused.

Times, dates and contact

The tension in the relationship between church ministers and funeral directors is often summed up around making contact. If I was to pick a visual symbol to illustrate this relationship it would be the telephone! Ministers speak of their deep frustration when funeral directors tell them of the date and time of a funeral as a fixed event, which often means that they are unable to help, while funeral directors talk of their annoyance when clergy don't answer the phone or get back quickly.

'As a funeral director, you want to get the date and time sorted as soon as possible. And if the vicar doesn't respond to the message, well, then you look elsewhere. There are plenty of other options available.'

Through our research and conversations we began to understand why fixing the date and time is so important to funeral directors. When families meet to plan the funeral they will usually spend between two and three hours in a meeting, and they have an expectation that by the time they leave the date and time of the funeral will have been finalized and they can begin to announce it. They may also have come with an idea of when they would like it to be – for example, later in the day to be convenient for friends and family to travel, or avoiding specific days for personal reasons. They may already have approached the venue for the wake and have made other preparations, or perhaps their friends can only come at a certain time. The funeral director's objective is to meet family needs, but they also have to pull together a number of factors including the availability of their staff, crematorium times, the celebrant – but above all, working with the family. The date and time of the funeral will be shared by the family as soon as they have finished the meeting, these days probably through social media, text or email – there is no need to wait for the copy date of the local paper as the only means of communication. During the meeting the funeral director will place a call with the church minister – vicar or Reader – and hope for it to be returned before the end of the meeting. If they haven't heard, they may then decide to take a risk and confirm the date and time with the family (unless the family have specified a particular celebrant or faith preference). So the vicar or Reader is presented with a fixed date. There is no easy solution to this issue, although understanding the problem and establishing good communication helps. Funeral directors particularly appreciate being up to date with contact details and ministers' availability around annual leave and days off.

Delivering good service

Another important concern for funeral directors relates to their expectations of the way in which the service itself is conducted, together with the support given to the family in planning and preparation. Funeral directors work to incredibly high standards of presentation and performance on the day, but ultimately trust the visible, public part of their business to someone else. The funeral is the last moment for the deceased to 'be in the spotlight' – it is, strangely, the ultimate 'live' event, with layers of expectations, and often laden with complications. Although none of us want to be part of a funeral where things go wrong, throughout the research there were stories of mistakes: the wrong name used consistently in the service, inaccurate facts related, and spelling mistakes.

The funeral director's reputation is dependent to a significant extent on what happens in the funeral service, so when ministers make mistakes it really matters. It upsets the family and it gives them the impression that the minister is not fully committed to the family's needs, which reflects on the funeral director.

'If I hadn't been upset I would have said, "Move the vicar out the way", 'cos he just got everything wrong … My dad was called Roland and he called him Ronald throughout the thing. I just wanted to say, "You're a lovely man, but I can get up and say …" He just got it wrong. He must have written things down wrong or something. So I was a bit … that was a bit disappointing.'

One funeral director from a family business talked of how in over 40 years of work he had never had a clergy person ask for feedback about the funeral. Not all funeral director staff will sit through services, but many staff from more traditional businesses will stay in the service. One curate heard us talking about the importance of feedback and decided to ask the local funeral director to give some feedback to him so that he could develop his funeral ministry further. The funeral director was delighted and from that contact a new level of relationship has grown.

It is not only content that makes an impact but also presentation:

'... the Church of England priest turned up and got out his laminated service sheets. It was such a visual demonstration of what is going wrong here. People today want a personalized service, they want to feel special, they want the uniqueness of their loved one to be captured somehow. The Church turns up with a wipe-clean, one-size-fits-all, standardized service ... probably still warm from its last use. How better to say, "We just don't really care about you, we just do the same thing for everyone."'

I wish I had made a note of the novel where I discovered this fabulous line: 'I find that undertakers prefer their clergy ironed.' It sums up the high standards of presentation that funeral directors expect, as they themselves work hard on appearance. A minister I met recently heard this and decided to make a real effort to smarten himself up (I don't know what his starting point was!) with highly polished shoes, clean, ironed surplice and so on. He noticed a difference in the way the local funeral directors responded to him; they were obviously appreciative, and it opened up the possibility of real conversation with them.

At the other extreme, the research showed that when a funeral is delivered well, funeral directors are delighted. Families will also speak about those who have really made an impression. It stands out when there is warmth, attention to detail and a real interest in the family and those attending the service. Funeral directors really appreciate those many clergy and Readers who put the feelings of the bereaved before their own attitudes.

'But the service was conducted by a lady vicar, priest – I'm not quite sure what she was. And she was lovely, actually ... I thought she struck a really nice tone. She was very relaxed. You didn't get the impression that she'd just polished someone else off before she started on this one ... She was very relaxed, as if she

had all the time in the world. *She obviously didn't know my aunt but she made it seem as if she'd known her, she would've liked her. So that felt nice, genuine, compassionate.'*

The way forward

If the picture that emerged from our research with funeral directors is somewhat negative, with a sense that the Church of England has a reputation for being badly organized, making mistakes and having rigid rules that hurt families, it equally transpired that there is some good news to celebrate. Many of us would like to find a simple, easy administrative solution to the communication problems that characterize the relationship between ministers and funeral directors. Several deaneries and dioceses are developing schemes that might help with the issue of availability: for example, a central phone number that can guarantee the availability of a minister at the proposed date and time, or a crematoria chaplaincy system, with different clergy taking turns to be available.

The research and conversations we had with funeral directors explored those ideas of central phone numbers, guaranteed ministers, and other practical schemes. The feedback suggested that systems are only part of the answer. In fact, the good news that emerged is that relationship is the biggest single factor in making a difference and building mutual understanding and respect. Funeral directors do not want a system that simply offers them an unknown 'minister' – they want to be sure that the person they have entrusted to take the funeral is going to do it as well as possible. Civil and independent celebrants spend considerable time on their training courses thinking about how to relate to the funeral director businesses in their locality. They have to engage in 'business-to-business' marketing to raise awareness of what they have to offer, but the best of them will also build good working relationships that are based on a common purpose – meeting the needs of the families they encounter.

It is this common purpose that provides the basis for working well with local funeral directors. The message to funeral directors is that we want to work with them to build good professional relationships, working together to ensure the needs of bereaved families in our area are met. There is a great deal of goodwill towards the Church of England among funeral professionals, but many of them express a sense that we do not communicate clearly all that we can offer, the vast experience that many of us have personally, the deep thought and wisdom we have available to us, and the centuries of serving families and reflecting on the big questions that arise around death.

> '*The church doesn't do enough to illustrate how it can help following bereavement, and then funeral directors are often too lazy or set in their ways to recommend clergy over other celebrants.*' (Funeral director)

Understanding each other

One key strategy encouraged during the pilot phase was building good relationships with funeral directors. Practical suggestions that emerged including popping in with cake for office staff (home-made cake always goes a long way to building friendships!), inviting appropriate staff to visit a church to see what a church funeral might actually involve, particularly if there is a resource there to hold the wake afterwards, offering training for new staff, and inviting them to induction services. This last suggestion is a really good idea, as alongside the local school, the funeral directors may be the people with whom the new vicar is going to work most frequently.

There is also a need to understand one another's work and working practices. Many clergy visited a funeral director during training or curacy, but taking an interest in a specific business, especially if asking for help in understanding new thinking and practices, can be much appreciated. Offering to spend time with staff explaining what is involved in a contemporary church-led service, sharing new resources and website information can all be valuable. But beyond this, it is good to listen to each other's concerns and pressures. The local funeral director is simply a small business (or a branch of a big business) with all the joys and stresses that brings, dealing with new technologies and legal frameworks, issues around poverty and payment, and any number of other local challenges. Likewise, a funeral director may not have any idea of the breadth of issues a local vicar is dealing with every week. The funeral director and their team are likely to be some of the few fellow professionals who can really understand the particular pressures of taking funerals, particularly those that are emotionally demanding. After the funeral of a child, for example, it is not just the vicar who feels the need to give their own child or grandchild an extra hug. The funeral director and the team will feel it too, so sharing those mutual feelings and thoughts can be part of a good relationship.

Prayer and care

There is also a place for offering good pastoral care and concern to the local funeral director. Include them in a regular prayer cycle in the parish calendar, or perhaps pay particular attention when there are tough situations to deal with. Many funeral directors employ young people as apprentices from age 18 onwards, and some of the situations they encounter can be very challenging, such as the death of a young person, or death in difficult circumstances. In the South West, one company providing training for young apprentice care workers uses GraveTalk to help them become comfortable in talking about death and dying with those they care for. GraveTalk may be a helpful tool in building relationship with the funeral director, particularly with younger employees. Having a good working relationship means that we can offer care and support, which may well be mutual.

Socializing turns out to have huge benefits. The Revd Juliet Stephenson, from Newcastle Diocese, won the Good Funeral Awards Funeral Celebrant of the Year award in 2015. It was not only bereaved families who nominated her but also local funeral directors and their staff. Juliet works really hard at building good relationships. When she left her previous parish, among many leaving parties, one was just for the staff from the local funeral director – around 15 people joined her for a pie and a pint night! When she arrived in her new parish, she again invited the teams out for drinks, getting to know them personally as well as professionally. It is also helpful to get to know the staff at the crematorium; although they are not directly involved in recommending celebrants, they do pass on their experiences and opinions to funeral directors.

We encouraged diocesan bishops from the pilot dioceses to host meetings to bring funeral directors and church ministers together, sometimes over a breakfast meeting. Many deaneries have annual meetings to share concerns with funeral directors, but the emphasis for these diocesan-level meetings was specific. When the bishop in one such meeting began his presentation by saying, 'I would simply like to thank you for the way you help families in this area,' those present visibly relaxed, as they realized they were being acknowledged as partners in the pastoral work that goes on around death and funerals. The meeting went on to give space for the airing of concerns and finding a commitment to better working together, but the initial words of thanks were much valued. Whether it happens at a parish, deanery or diocesan level, working together with funeral directors to build relationships can be immensely helpful in enabling the church to minister effectively to bereaved families in their area.

During the pilot phase a number of ministers shared at feedback groups their experience of focusing on a relationship with the funeral director. Some felt that the new resources helped them to have interesting and fresh conversations with funeral directors, whereas others changed how they responded to enquiries:

> *'I do answer things a lot quicker than I did before. I just think I'm more mindful of their [the funeral director's] position than I was.'*

Several ministers experienced an increase in the number of funerals they were asked to be involved with, and in one parish that led to pressure on resources as the numbers rose dramatically. For others it was a steady but noticeable change in attitude that began to make an impact.

> *'I think that since we've been doing this and really focusing on the energy, because we make life easier for them, because they're beginning to believe that we will always say yes, they "point our way" more often.'*

While the research conducted nationally has shown some clear patterns and possibilities around the relationship between church and funeral directors, it is not the same everywhere. There is huge variation across the country in attitudes and practice. But there is good evidence that unless the Church of England finds a way to work effectively with local funeral directors it will be increasingly difficult to meet families at one of the most significant moments in life – a close bereavement. This means making sure that there is awareness of what we offer, good communication and a willingness to work together to create practical solutions to the pressures we are all facing.

5 Consistent follow-up and after-care make a difference

Remembering the bereaved

Whenever we present the key messages about funerals to clergy and Readers, we ask if any of them know of people in their congregation who are there because of bereavement. There is always a near 100 per cent positive response. That does not necessarily mean that the contact has come directly through a recent funeral taken by a minister from that church. Bereaved people are sometimes drawn to church months or even years after a death has occurred, as part of the journey of grief and the questions that it has raised for them, and possibly because churches have specialist groups or individuals who offer bereavement support. Being there for people after a funeral does not have to involve creating specially trained teams of people, however, but may be more about how warmth and welcome are offered by a community.

In the episode mentioned earlier from the hit BBC comedy *Car Share* (series 1, episode 2), a conversation takes place, referring to John's own recent experience of a funeral:

> *In the car. Red light. The traffic stops.*
>
> JOHN   My dad wanted 'Three Steps to Heaven', Eddie Cochrane, when he died. They brought his coffin into church …
>
> KAYLEIGH   Your dad's dead?
>
> JOHN   Yeah.
>
> KAYLEIGH   But you talk about him all the time. When did he die?
>
> JOHN   Just before Christmas.
>
> KAYLEIGH   Sorry. I never knew.
>
> JOHN   I were off work for a month. You signed me sympathy card.
>
> KAYLEIGH   Oh yeah. Yeah, I remember now. Aww, must have been an awful time.
>
> JOHN   It's all right. He'd been ill for ages. [*beat*] Why do people always say it's all right when … it isn't all right. He'd been ill for ages but it was still shit when it happened.

As with so much excellent comedy, there is both humour and seriousness within this short extract. The language that people use around grief and loss may try to minimize the impact, and there is this sense that life goes on for the rest of the world, illustrated by Kayleigh's forgetfulness of John's bereavement. It helps to remind us that underpinning our response to those who are bereaved, whether or not we have been involved with the funeral, is a need for careful listening and attention.

Much of the language and interaction in the planning and leading of a funeral will focus on those who have been closest to the deceased, and in particular those who are organizing the funeral. They are sometimes identified by funeral directors as the 'chief mourner', maybe the close family who walk alongside the coffin, or those for whom seats are reserved. But it is likely that there will be many more bereaved people at the funeral, and it may be that this wider group live in the local parish. An elderly widow who had lived next door to the same family for 50 or more years, becoming lifelong friends, died recently. Her children and grandchildren travelled a long way to come to the service, but will not often return to the parish afterwards other than to sort out practical things. But her neighbours will miss her, and as people get older the loss of friends can be very difficult, so it may be that these are the people who would welcome an invitation to church or an enquiry about how they are feeling. Likewise, being the last remaining child in one generation can stir up huge feelings, and yet it is the kind of grief that may be overlooked as attention focuses on younger generations. Sometimes a tragic death sends ripples through a community, reminding people of their own mortality or rekindling emotions about previous losses. I was vicar in a parish where a young girl died through a tragic accident. Her immediate family did not live in the community, but the impact on the school, on the neighbours, on everyone in the local area, meant that there was a need to address grief and loss beyond those identified as 'chief mourners'.

Understanding grief

Grief is a normal human response to being bereaved, and although sometimes it is necessary to seek specialist help and care, most of the time it is a journey made in the company of kindness, compassion and friendship. It is also a long journey. Sometimes the impression given in the media is that the loss of someone is felt intensely for a while, but then the script moves on, and the situation is forgotten. This is particularly true in some TV soaps, where traumatic, tragic deaths occur but within a few days or weeks life has returned to normal. The reality is that once we are bereaved, we are always bereaved, although the intensity of grief may fade. People may worry that their particular experience of grief is not 'normal', or express a view that they should be 'over it' within a certain time-frame, whereas the reality may go way beyond the first year. A BBC documentary exploring the impact of grief, particularly on young husbands and fathers (the documentary itself is part of the emerging public conversation about death and dying talked about earlier), was aired in Spring

2017, with the acknowledgement that grief takes time. This was echoed in a 'Thought for the Day' on Radio 4's *Today* programme.

> *Somehow we've ended up almost privatizing bereavement so that on the morning after the funeral it can sometimes seem to the bereaved that they are being left to get on with it by themselves as the rest of us, with our ineptitude around death, prefer to keep mum … We really never ought to assume that someone else's mourning is over and done with.* (Michael Banner, 'Thought for the Day', 2017)

Throughout the research interviews, it emerged that after a while people can begin to feel that they are frustrating or burdening family and friends with their needs. Several spoke of needing to talk to somebody who understood what they were going through. Although some had turned to doctors or counsellors for help, this is also the moment when support from the local church through kindness and friendship can be really valued. In Lichfield diocese, one response to the insights that emerged from the research has been to encourage congregations to become 'death confident'. Part of this means becoming the kind of people who are readily able to reach out, listen and talk as friends and neighbours with those who may be grieving in the community. Jane decided to hold an 'open coffee morning' once a month in her home, inviting neighbours to come along. Sometimes there are just three or four, sometimes more. She has discovered that many of those who come need to share stories of bereavement, not necessarily recent, but still central to their lives. When the time is right, she may invite them to something else, gently introducing them to church and faith, but otherwise simply being compassionate and loving, living out the good news of hope in Jesus Christ.

Much has been written about grief and bereavement, so if a church is setting up a ministry focused on offering this support there will be courses and books to choose from, including those from a faith perspective. For example, both Cruse and Care for the Family have excellent programmes that could help those interested in providing support, as well as providing support themselves for those who are bereaved. Some churches may well be involved in a real ministry around offering formal bereavement groups or individual care. For others it may just be about becoming aware and confident in offering friendship and welcome.

> '*The Church supports people through grief and loss by being alongside, when they are wanted. It's a complicated process. And everyone grieves differently; we all know that from our own experience. I think there's all sorts of things we can do. The fact that we're a loving community means that there can be people from within the church who will visit and just sit and listen, have a cup of tea. There can be post-bereavement groups in some places.*' (Archbishop Justin Welby)

Keeping in contact: Making the first move

Throughout all our research around life events, whether baptism, weddings or funerals, one universal finding was that people really don't mind us keeping in touch after the event; this gives them a choice as to how to respond. For some that contact is enough, whereas for others, hearing from the church leads to a response and a step towards belonging. Perhaps more than with other life events, it can feel difficult to continue with contact after a funeral; many of our clergy and Reader groups expressed anxiety about being perceived as intrusive or pushy. Our involvement in funeral ministry is motivated primarily by compassion, reflecting the heart of God that is moved by grief and loss. Rightly, we are anxious to avoid any sense of exploiting grief or preying on those who may be particularly vulnerable. However, the research helped us to understand that our reserve may be understood as a lack of interest, particularly by those who have not been regular members of a congregation.

> '*If you're a churchgoer the chances are the vicar will stop to say, "Hello, how are you today?" But, if you're not a churchgoer, the chances of the vicar stopping … to speak to you are fairly remote. And I think the church have got something to learn in that respect, in relation to the selection of people for the ministry, and the way that they train their staff to come across in a pastoral sense, rather than just being – shall we say – a little bit aloof.*'

One of the strangest blessings in my own ministry has turned out to be that I grew up with one parent who was afraid of the local vicar, and one parent who treated everyone as a potential friend. It was my mother who was anxious about the vicar. It wasn't personal, as there were at least three during my childhood years, but whenever the vicar came into the village shop, which we ran, my mum would call one of us to come and serve him. So I have always known that not everyone finds the idea of a visit from a vicar a treat, and that not everyone will find it easy to pick up the phone or knock on the vicarage door for a chat. From an adult perspective I now understand that much of this anxiety was rooted in a sense that the vicar is a highly educated person who often lives in a big house, an anxiety that still prevails today. It is also the case that when we are grieving we may feel particularly vulnerable, so that taking social risks and stepping into new situations can become difficult. This was reflected in our research as people talked about where contact was initiated after the funeral:

> 'I suppose that if I'd gone to see him and said, "Can I sit and talk?" he'd have been very good … If he'd contacted me and said, "How are you coping? Are you okay?" I probably would have said to him, "No, I'm not, can I come down and see you to talk? I need to get this out in the open."'

This is an extract from a much longer interview, where the respondent talked of the difficulty in summoning up the energy and the courage to make contact with the vicar, even though she really wanted to talk. A proactive approach may have given the opportunity to share feelings, although equally it may not. Often a local church makes contact once or twice, and then stops if the person has not been seen at a service, perhaps worried that we might seem too pushy or that the lack of visible response indicates that someone is not interested. All our research has shown consistently that it can take a long time to move from receiving information to acting on it, so keeping in touch needs to be both consistent and continuous. As with other life events, keeping in touch needs to be focused and appropriate, with invitations to specific events rather than simply sending the parish magazine. For some people, coming to church will mean that they are looking for conversation and contact, people to talk to, company and conversation, which may happen in social events as much as around worship.

> 'It's much more formal at church and it makes you feel much more relaxed at the chapel. They all seem to be your friends: very nice feeling.'

For others in our research there was a more inarticulate sense of simply being in the space that a church offers, finding that this in itself brings some sense of hope and comfort. People might value being able to access a church during the day, perhaps being able to place something on a prayer tree or prayer board, or, where appropriate, light a candle.

'Here it is, and you're welcome; they welcome everybody in, and you probably feel that's there, and that will hopefully do some good. And if it doesn't do much good, it shouldn't do too much harm.'

This means that the ministry of welcome is incredibly important, as is being able to discern the appropriate level of engagement, providing space when needed, and also offering to get alongside those who need support. This was vividly illustrated for me when I went to the local church on the Sunday before my mother's funeral. I was not in a good place, as both my parents had died suddenly within the previous six months, and as the first hymn ('Be thou my vision') began, I simply began to weep. I was alone in the pew, and I could positively feel the frisson of anxiety around me – what to do with a middle-aged woman crying in church? So they did absolutely nothing. In contrast, a friend described a very similar moment in a Quaker meeting. As she began to weep in the silent stillness, the person sitting next to her simply placed a hand on top of hers, showing empathy and support, and above all, awareness.

If we are going to reach out and welcome the bereaved into church, then it is a ministry of the whole people of God, with all of us aware of our responsibility to be open and sensitive. As someone who visits many different churches, I could tell so many stories about welcome – even though I have yet to meet the church that describes itself as unfriendly! I have come across a huge range of different approaches, ranging from the negligent to the excellent, and I often imagine what it would be like if I were a grieving widow or widower.

I visited one church that had box pews (including brass nameplates) and a small congregation. A handful of books and notices was thrust into my hand. No one spoke to me, although there was plenty of chatter around me. I inadvertently sat in the front – about halfway down one side. The service was very short and swift, lasting no more than 45 minutes including hymns and sermon, leaving me no room to catch my thoughts or prayers. No one spoke to me at the end, and as I left I realized that they had no idea whether I had just moved in locally, was a grieving person, or had recently won the lottery and was deciding where to give my money!

In contrast, there is Margaret. Margaret is in her eighties and used to be a pub landlady, which may explain why she is so good at welcome. On this particular Sunday, a visitor arrived for the first time at church, and Margaret accompanied her to find a seat, and sat with her – even though it was the front row, which would not be her personal preference. As the visitor had English as a second language, Margaret went to a great deal of trouble to help her through the service, pointing things out, even whispering as needed. Afterwards she brought the visitor for coffee, taking time to introduce her to others, and her only worry was whether she had been helpful enough: 'I wish I hadn't let her go first to communion. She should have followed me so she could see what to do.'

The good news is that several months later that visitor still comes to church and is now involved in helping with the offertory herself, having become part of the community. Across all the research around life events it became clear that welcome and friendship shown by the congregation is really important in creating a positive experience of church, which may make all the difference when the next opportunity for contact with God and God's people comes along.

Invitational, intentional follow-up

Of the many different ways to keep in touch, it may well be that sending cards at regular intervals is one of the most helpful, particularly after bereavement when cards and notes are much appreciated. Cards are often sent to those who are closest to the person who has died – spouses, children – but it may sometimes be appropriate to send cards to those outside that circle who may have been deeply impacted by the death. This can be particularly true for those who are single, where friends rather than family may be needing particular sympathy and support.

Sympathy cards are often taken down and put away around a month after the death, and it's at that point that expectations that life will go on as before can surface. Family and friends go back to their usual activities, and the adjustments begin to be made. Sending a card at this point to remind the family that the church has not forgotten them can be very helpful. Some also like to send a card on the first and second anniversary of death, and this might be accompanied by an invitation to a church service where their special person will be remembered by name. During the pilot phase of the research we tested out a range of cards, adapting them in response to feedback from church ministers and families. There is a simple selection available (see www.churchprinthub.org), all of which can be overprinted with church contact details, and the Pastoral Services Diary (www.pastoralservicesdiary.org) is a way of maintaining contact information so that the cards are sent at appropriate times. The birthday of the deceased can be a significant day with real poignancy, and this online reminder system allows this to be entered as a date when a card might be appreciated, which may well make a big impact, as few outside the family may realize the importance of the date. The fact that we don't extend an invitation or offer a welcome may reinforce the impression some people have that we are not interested, and that church is not really for them after all.

> *'If you have a vicar within your own area, there should be a follow-up. My experience was there was no follow-up from the Church of England for my wife's funeral. [It makes you feel like] the Church of England aren't as friendly.'*

Follow-up is the bridge from mission to discipleship. We may not see people again after a funeral. It may be that our contact is part of a journey to Jesus that takes years, and happens in another location altogether. But what we have discovered from all our research is that keeping in touch opens up the possibility; if we don't keep in contact, then we are limiting opportunities for a life-changing relationship to flourish. The journey of grief may be long, and bereavement is permanent. The Church is there for as long as a person needs us, wherever they go. We are there with space, compassion, prayer and support, simply reflecting the hospitality of God for those in need.

The journey to remembering

Many churches have noticed, in recent years, that attendance at any form of service that involves remembering those we love but see no longer has been increasing. I know of parishes that regularly report that the congregation at an annual 'All Souls' service will be around a hundred, and as well as those for whom they have taken funerals, many others attend from the community as word spreads. People often return each year – and will come to the church where they live even if the funeral happened in a different parish. One of our respondents talked of how an invitation arrived from the church many miles away where her parents' funeral had been held, but she discovered that a similar service happened in her local church and went along. Keeping in touch may have an impact that we may never learn about.

There is an interesting piece of research waiting to be done exploring the correlation between the growth in the funeral as an occasion of celebration and the growth of 'remembering' services. Although loss and grief may be mini-malized at the funeral service itself, or brushed aside, this does not mean that they are minimalized in the experience of the bereaved. It's all very well to sit through a funeral with Fred's friends and family saying how marvellous he was, and what a jolly good chap he was, and laughing at all the stories, but six months later Fred's widow is still a widow. The jolly friends have gone and she is left with all the mixed emotions of remembering him. She may feel angry at times that he has left her, deeply sad at the loss of the future that isn't coming into being, or sometimes glad that she has so many good memories. Into this maelstrom of emotion a little card drops through the door inviting her to a special service to remember. In that service she doesn't have to feel or be anything in particular. She can weep or rage or smile, perhaps light a candle and be surrounded by the comfort of a community and a message of hope. These kinds of services have become an important part of the journey of grief and bereavement, and also represent an important part of an ongoing relationship.

It is not only the Church that initiates opportunities for remembering:

'Then around Christmas time they sent us a little star [Christmas decoration] to do with Christmas, and you could write a little thing on there. And then they had a service at one of the local churches, and you had a tree there, and every-one that had lost somebody in that year could go down.'

This refers to contact being made from the funeral director, although the remembering service was held in a local church, so this may be one area where church and funeral directors can work together. Increasingly, funeral directors are staying in contact after the ceremony, offering the extended support that meets families' needs; it also helps to secure their business reputation. Funeral directors sometimes offer counselling services (hence the presence of bereavement organizations at the National Funeral Exhibition) and organize special annual services to remember loved ones. The research showed that these gestures are widely appreciated, and reinforce respect and regard for the funeral director and all that they do.

The Church traditionally offers such services in the season where theo-logically, biblically and liturgically we begin to think about end times and the life that is to come. This has come to be called the 'Kingdom season', and around the beginning of November we invite people to join us for 'All Souls' commemorations. In many parishes this will then flow seamlessly into the following week and Remembrance Sunday, which is set aside for remembering those who have lost their lives in human conflict. For some, their particular story of loss may mean that both occasions are important. For most bereaved people certain dates in the community or public calendar carry a great deal of significance, the most obvious being Christmas – nearly everyone who has been bereaved will talk of how Christmas is difficult. The dissonance between a commercial and cultural message that says that Christmas has to be the Best, the Happiest, the most Loving day of the year, and the feelings of loss and grief can be very marked. Some churches in our pilot, and others throughout the country, have begun to acknowledge this, holding services near Christmas that offer space for the bereaved and others to reflect. One such service is known as 'Blue Christmas' (see churchsupporthub.org/funerals/ideas for details), and one church that holds such a service reports around 75–100 people who come to sit quietly with a simple liturgy, a couple of carols and time to pray.

But Christmas is not the only occasion when bereaved people can feel at odds with the mood of celebration that the culture is promoting. Mothering Sunday is a day when many churches make sure that they include space for sadness and regret alongside thanksgiving. Fewer churches recognize Father's Day or Valentine's Day, but these are both days that can be emotional in the journey of grief.

If you have just lost your life partner of 40, 50 or 60 years, then the hype around the celebration of romantic love can emphasize your isolation. One of the most realistic moments in BBC Radio 4's *The Archers* came in February 2016, when Bert talked of 'his Freda' on Valentine's Day, the first since her death. The Church can offer a different space around these public occasions, finding new ways to meet the needs of bereaved families. Including appropriate symbols is really important, perhaps especially the lighting of a candle, which is both a reminder of the light of Christ and a sign of prayer. As part of a ministry around funerals, building relationship and making connections, it is also good to offer hospitality after such a service, including refreshments. Sending specific invitations for these services as well as other church events helps people to feel supported and connected. It may be helpful to remind people that they can light a candle online on the funerals website, which is another way of praying and being in contact with church.

Ashes and memorialization

Among the many changes that have emerged in the past 20 years or so, different ways have emerged in which people wish to remember their loved ones. Now that 70 per cent of funerals are cremations, the disposal of ashes has become ever more important. For some families it will naturally follow on closely after the funeral service, perhaps even on the same day, but for others this final act may be delayed until a significant day, when the family feel ready, or it may never happen at all. Crematoria and funeral directors all note that there are ashes that are never collected.

> *There is considerable confusion in people's minds as to what can be done with people's ashes. Cremated remains are often disposed of in a favourite place of the person who has died, which may be a hillside, or by a favourite lake, or on the pitch of the person's favourite football team. However, the canons of the Church of England state that cremated remains should be disposed of in a churchyard or burial ground or area of land so designated by a bishop, or at sea – no other option is given.* (Jeremy Brooks, *Heaven's Morning Breaks*, p. 123)

Our research noted that this can be a difficult moment, often fraught with family tensions and worries about what is acceptable, not just from a church perspective, but perhaps in a more general moral or ethical sense. Under Church of England canon law, ashes must be strewn (that is, poured directly into the ground) or buried in a casket, but this gives no guidance as to what a minister might offer as prayers in other circumstances, and there are now many more options available to families around the disposal of ashes.

One significant new practice that is emerging is the placing of ashes in items such as jewellery, or embedded into glass.

> *Cremation jewellery: we have a wide range of silver, gold and ashes within glass jewellery that is designed to contain some of your loved one's ashes. By turning a small amount of ashes into jewellery you can keep your loved one with you for ever. They make beautiful sympathy gifts as well as heirloom pieces that can be handed down the generations … All our cremation jewellery is very discreet so you can tell people if you want or just be comforted in the knowledge that they are with you when you need them.* (www.scatteringashes.co.uk)

One reason for this reluctance to bury ashes may be the increasingly mobile nature of the population. Once ashes are buried (or indeed a body) that place will be permanent, and it is extremely rare for permission to be given for exhumation. So for some people, having a way of taking cremated remains with them in the future may be important. For others, being able to disperse ashes in what is perceived as an organic or natural way matters, and there are many creative options available (see www.scatteringashes.co.uk)

A further change has emerged in the world of the digital legacy: your online presence after your death. People want to honour their loved one's memory in various ways, but may become anxious about social media legacy, such as Facebook pages. Church ministers simply need to be aware that these are issues that may need to be addressed and approached with pastoral sensitivity.

A further task after the funeral involves the erecting of a headstone or memorial stone to mark a grave or ashes plot. The scope of this research did not include talking to bereaved people about this issue, but practically the advice we have developed recommends a clear and strong statement as early as possible that burial in a churchyard will have implications for the design of any stone.

Conclusion: Taking funerals seriously

The title of our first national conference in 2015 and subsequent day conferences to dioceses emerged directly from conversations with funeral professionals who used this exact phrase as we began to talk with them: 'I'm so glad that the Church of England is taking funerals seriously again.' The implication is that over past decades changes have happened, new practices and ideas have emerged, and the Church of England has not always responded. This work, commissioned, funded and overseen by the Archbishops' Council, is a step towards engaging effectively with the thousands of people we meet each year through this ministry. Ministry to the bereaved and preparing the dying for their death have always been core practices for Christians, and we now face the challenge of reimagining that ministry for the twenty-first century in the changing culture of England.

It is such an important ministry that underpinning it with prayer has been a key part of the local church's support to those who have been bereaved in the community. In some churches this means regularly including the names of the recently deceased in the prayer notices, perhaps for a month or so around the funeral. Others will also remember anniversaries for one or more years. But it may be worth considering more focused prayer around funeral ministry, identifying a team of people who will pray not only for specific situations but for all those involved, including funeral directors, musicians, ministers, as well as family and friends.

Our key messages are that we have an amazing opportunity to be part of an emerging conversation around death and dying, and we need to have confidence in what we do and what we have to share. We have real skills and distinctive experience to bring to funeral ministry, but we need to recognize that contemporary funerals have to build bridges from the personal to the sacred as we share the good news of God's love in Jesus. We need to build relationships – perhaps especially professional relationships with funeral directors and their staff, and we need to become more proactive in explaining what we offer and how we help. Finally we need to have courage to keep in contact, to follow up consistently so that those we meet have an opportunity to discover the transforming presence of Jesus.

There were key steps in the funeral journey, steps that begin even before death has happened as we get people talking and planning. Once a point of need arrives, we have a real opportunity to meet with the bereaved and to support them with prayer before the service itself happens. On the day, we offer pastoral care and prayer opportunities, before supporting through grief and remembering for as long as we are needed. The amazing thing about the Church of England is that we are there whenever people need us, wherever they go, with no time limits. Jesus met people in all kinds of life circumstances, including funerals, and when he did his presence transformed the situation from a day of hopelessness into one of hopefulness. The Church of England continues to minister the transforming presence of Jesus to thousands of people, and that transforming presence continues to make a difference every step of the way.

SIX SPECIAL MOMENTS

Here are six key opportunities for a church who wants to develop their ministry around funerals. It starts with encouraging conversations around funeral plans, and then moves through key moments around the funeral itself.

1. **Plan** – use the Church of England 'My Funeral Plans' booklet to encourage people to write down wishes.
2. **Inform** – share the Church of England website (churchofenglandfunerals. org) with funeral directors and families with a card or leaflet.
3. **Pray** – offer families a special card at the funeral visit, assuring them of the church's prayer and support.
4. **Involve** – give the congregation a prayer card so they can continue to pray after the service.
5. **Support** – send sympathy and anniversary cards as appropriate to show care and interest.
6. **Invite** – send invitations to special times of remembering whenever they happen, for as long as is appropriate.

TEN TOP TIPS

Alongside the six special moments, here are some tips for good practice around funeral ministry. These reflect insights from research and experience so the local church can grow in confidence in reaching out to the bereaved, build good relationships with families and professionals, and have the courage to make small changes that will help families whenever and wherever they need us.

1. **Build relationships with funeral directors** – offer tea, prayer and training: work together to serve the families in your communities.
2. **Get involved in the emerging public conversation about death and dying** and encourage people to write down their funeral wishes.
3. **Make sure there is information about Church of England-led funerals** in any local places where people might look, including funeral directors and crematoria.
4. **Be warm and personal**, smile and listen well to the personal story that is being told.

5 **Offer prayer support** from the moment you meet, being mindful of the time gap between the visit and the funeral.

6 **Be confident in offering spiritual care** and invite people to pray before, at and after the event.

7 **Remember the transforming presence of Jesus** and offer a message of comfort and hope.

8 **Give the whole congregation confidence** to be part of offering ongoing bereavement care through kindness and neighbourliness.

9 **Send cards and invitations** to specific activities and events, not just worship services, but places where people can meet people.

10 **Hold special remembering services** at Christmas and other occasions during the year.

Part Five

Afterword, resources and taking it further

Afterword

What next for the Life Events work?

The Life Events team is now busy encouraging parishes throughout the Church of England to value and enjoy ministry with those we meet through what some may think of as traditional parish ministry – baptisms, weddings and funerals. We are challenging dioceses and parishes to recognize the importance of building good relationships and doing consistent follow-up and helping them to access the tools and resources that will support them – many of which are outlined later in this final part of the book.

The team continues to make presentations to dioceses and specialist conferences, and is also working to help dioceses support parishes at a local level. Long-term research about impact is being done in three dioceses and new workshops and online training material will soon be available. There is a need to share key insights with those who are training for different forms of ministry and for those who have been in ministry for some while. Alongside this we continue to monitor and research experience and expectations of the Christian faith and the Church of England in our contemporary culture, so that we can help the Church to proclaim the good news in fresh ways to each generation, as people encounter those life-changing moments around the birth of a child, marriage and the death of someone they love.

When people realize the numbers of contacts that are made and the opportunities that arise for conversation with people who may otherwise have very little to do with the church, then confidence begins to grow. As fewer people have any history of churchgoing or residual memory of the story of Jesus, this early contact enables the Church to show the kind of hospitality and care that can help them on their own journey of faith, at whatever point we meet them.

Ministering to those we meet through one of life's big moments is also where those who are already on their faith journey and active in a local church can grow their faith as they pray for all involved and commit to being part of showing welcome and warmth. That may be within the context of church services and activities, or in a more specific ministry such as baptism or marriage preparation, toddler groups, bereavement support, pastoral visiting and other ways of serving. The national resources for Life Events are helping to support local parishes by providing high-quality messages that help both those who come to us and those who welcome them to see that they are part of something much bigger, and that wherever they or their family are in England, there will be a local church there ready to show God's love and share the good news of Jesus Christ. My prayer and my passion, together with the prayers and passion and skills of those who work as part of the Life Events team, is that as we offer people our help, experience and hospitality at their special moment, so their lives will be transformed as the lifelong journey of relationship with God through Jesus unfolds for them. Amen!

Useful books, organizations and websites

Books referred to in the text

Baptism

Laura Barnett, *The Versions of Us*, Weidenfeld and Nicolson, 2015.

Jacqui Hyde, *We Welcome You: Baptism Preparation with Families*, Church House Publishing, 2016.

Timothy Radcliffe, *Taking the Plunge*, Bloomsbury Continuum, 2012.

Jenny Paddison, *Starting Rite: Spiritual Nurture for Babies and their Parents*, Church House Publishing, 2015.

Weddings

Gillian Oliver, *The Church Weddings Handbook*, Church House Publishing, 2012.

Funerals

Jeremy Brooks, *Heaven's Morning Breaks*, Kevin Mayhew, 2013.

Douglas Davies, *Mors Britannica: Lifestyle and Death-style in Britain Today*, Oxford University Press, 2015.

Douglas Davies and Hannah Rumble, *Natural Burial*, Continuum, 2012.

Ewan Kelly, *Meaningful Funerals*, Mowbray, 2008.

Liturgy

Common Worship: Christian Initiation, Church House Publishing, 2006.

Common Worship Christian Initiation: Additional Baptism Texts in Accessible Language, Church House Publishing, 2015.

Common Worship: Pastoral Services, Church House Publishing, 2000.

Common Worship: Services and Prayers for the Church of England, Church House Publishing, 2000.

Sandra Millar, *Festivals Together*, SPCK, 2012.

Sandra Millar, *Worship Together*, SPCK, 2012.

General

Charles Duhigg, *The Power of Habit*, Random House, 2013.

John Pritchard, *Something More*, SPCK, 2016.

KPMG, 'Making Memories', Nunwood, 2016.

Barna Group, 'Talking Jesus', Evangelical Alliance, Church of England and Hope UK, 2015 (free download).

Organizations referred to in the text

The Child Bereavement Trust: www.childbereavement.org
Supports families and professionals when a baby or child dies. Includes a special section for young people.

Cruse Bereavement Care: www.cruse.org.uk
Includes information about local services.

CARE for the family: www.careforthefamily.org.uk
Includes sections on parent support, marriage support and bereavement support and information about courses.

Other useful resources

Baptism

The Baptism Cube, Church House Publishing, 2006.

Ally Barrett, *Making the Most of Your Child's Baptism*, SPCK, 2016.

Mark Earey, Trevor Lloyd and Ian Tarrant (eds), *Connecting with Baptism*, Church House Publishing, 2007.

Richard Burge, Penny Fuller, Mary Hawes and Jo Williams, *Getting Ready for Baptism* Course Book and Activity Book, Barnabas, 2004 (for children aged 5 and over).

Simon Jones, *Celebrating Christian Initiation*, Alcuin Club, 2016.

Lucy Moore, *Messy Church*, BRF, 2011.

Helen Sammon, 'We want to get the baby done', *Church Times*, 9 September 2011.

Church of England Education Office, 'Rooted in the Church', 2016.

Weddings and marriage

Ally Barrett, *Making the Most of Your Church Wedding*, SPCK, 2014.

Nicky and Sila Lee, *The Marriage Book*, Alpha, 2009.

Mark Oakley, *Readings for Weddings*, SPCK, 2013.

Death and funerals

Robert Atwell, *Peace at the Last*, Canterbury Press, 2014.

Sue Brayne, *The D-Word*, Bloomsbury, 2010.

Ruth Burgess, *Saying Goodbye*, Wild Goose Publications, 2013.

Marian Carter, *Dying to Live*, SCM Press, 2014.

John James and Russell Friedman, *The Grief Recovery Handbook*, 2009.

Peter Jupp, *Death, Our Future*, Epworth, 2008.

Paul Kalanithi, *When Breath Becomes Air*, Penguin, 2016.

Thomas G. Long and Thomas Lynch, *The Good Funeral*, Westminster John Knox, 2013.

Brendan McCarthy and others, *At the End of the Day*, Church House Publishing, 2014.

Life Events

Mark Oakley, *Readings for Funerals*, SPCK, 2015.
Stephen Oliver, *Inside Grief*, SPCK, 2013.
Lezley J. Stewart, *Celebrating Life in Death*, Saint Andrew Press, 2016.
Tony Walter, *Funerals and How to Improve Them*, Hodder and Stoughton, 1990.
David Winter, *At the End of the Day*, BRF, 2013.

General

Alan Billings, *Secular Lives, Sacred Hearts*, SPCK, 2004.
Alan Billings, *Lost Church*, SPCK, 2013.
Andrew Brown and Linda Woodhead, *That Was The Church That Was*, Bloomsbury, 2016.
Wesley Carr, *Brief Encounters*, SPCK, 1985.
Michael Morpurgo, *Singing for Mrs Pettigrew*, Walker Books, 2007.
Mark Oakley, *The Splash of Words: Believing in Poetry*, Canterbury Press, 2016.
Russ Parker, *Rediscovering the Ministry of Blessing*, SPCK, 2013.
Sam Wells, *How Then Shall We Live*, Canterbury Press, 2016.

Useful organizations

The Spiritual Child: www.spiritualchild.co.uk
Information and ideas for supporting spiritual life in children and families.

Messy Church: www.messychurch.org .uk
Ideas and resources about one approach to involving families in a new way of being church.

1277: www.1277.org.uk
Website with information about church-led toddler groups, how to set up and keep going.

Mothers' Union: www.themothersunion.org
Lots of information about marriage, family life, children and church.

ROOTS: www.rootsontheweb.org
Ideas and resources for Sunday worship for children, families and all ages.

Websites developed by the Life Events team

The Life Events team has developed a range of websites. Three of these are aimed at those who are looking to have a service to mark a life event, and three provide resources for parishes in their ministry.

Websites to point people to

www.churchofenglandchristenings.org
This website was launched in 2013 and has all the information that parents and others need when they begin to think about having a child christened. It contains practical suggestions for encouraging families on the amazing journey of faith as well as an outline of the service itself. There are four main sections:

- **A parent's guide to christenings** – how to find a church, what it means to have a child baptized at a christening, the option of a thanksgiving service, who needs to be involved, and the content of the service. It includes a walk-through of the service.
- **A godparent's guide to christenings** – godparents have a very special role to play, so this section helps to answer their specific questions, outlining what it means, who can be a godparent, ideas on gifts and what happens in the service.
- **A guest's guide to christenings** – for people invited to a christening who may never have been to one before, this gives information and advice on what happens, practicalities about children, gifts, photographs and much more.
- **After the christening** – this is the largest section on the site and is packed with ideas to help families continue the amazing journey of faith after the

day. It includes ideas for prayers, Bible stories to read, fun ideas to enjoy God's world, craft activities and much more.

There are two additional features:

- **Next Steps** – this is an e-newsletter that comes out four times a year, designed to help parents engage with faith and church in the months and years after the christenings. It is immensely practical, written by experts in church and family and encourages contact with the local church. Parents can sign up directly on the site.

- **Light a candle** – this is an interactive section of the site that allows a person to light a candle to remember a child who is being baptized. It is thoughtful and can be taken at the pace set by the user. No personal information is entered, but it can be shared on the user's own social media accounts. It is a great alternative to being able to light a candle in a church.

www.yourchurchwedding.org

This website was created around eight years ago, and has recently been redesigned to make it fully usable on mobile devices. It is a very comprehensive site that is well worth recommending to couples. The extensive content is grouped under four key headings:

- **Just engaged** – where couples can find answers to all the legal and practical questions that they have about getting married in church, including how to find a church, legal requirements, practical concerns and much more.

- **Planning your ceremony** – all the information needed about the service itself, including a walk-through guide, hymns to listen to, readings to choose from, choices to be made. There is information about photography, choreography, rehearsals, children and much more. There is a special area called 'The ceremony planner' where couples can enter their choices, and print out a draft service to discuss with their vicar.

- **More about marriage** – shaped around the core words from the unique vows said at a church wedding, this section helps couples begin to think about the difference being married might make to their lives. It can act as a guide for marriage preparation or the basis for a discussion, or offer advice well into the future after the wedding day.

- **Guests and special roles** – information for bridesmaids, best man, readers, or simply those who have been invited and may never have attended a church wedding before.

www.churchofenglandfunerals.org
This website was launched in 2015 and provides help and information for anyone wanting to understand what happens at a Church of England-led funeral. It is useful for funeral directors as well as bereaved individuals and those who want to make some plans about their own funeral. It includes:

- **Here for you** – a general introduction to what is distinctive about a Church of England funeral including a message of hope.
- **Organizing a funeral** – practical information that people need when someone has recently died, including sections on finding a minister, finding a church and guidance as to what happens in the service itself. There is also a separate service walk-through, which includes hymns to listen to and choose from and a selection of readings, both biblical and other appropriate suggestions.
- **Going to a funeral** – information especially designed to help those who may be going to a funeral for the first time. Also includes help for taking part as a reader, and how to support a grieving person.
- **After the funeral** – information and advice on the practical questions around ashes and memorials, remembering services and bereavement support with lots of contact information.
- **My funeral plans** – information on how to make sure people know of choices that can be made in advance, encouraging people to select hymns, readings and think through other information that may be needed.
- **Light a candle** – an interactive section of the site that allows a person to light a candle to remember a loved one. It is thoughtful and can be taken at the pace set by the user. No personal information is entered, but it can be shared on the user's own social media accounts. It is a great alternative to being able to light a candle in a church.

Websites to help churches

churchsupporthub.org

The team wanted to create a website where clergy, Readers, licensed ministers and lay people with interest or special roles could find information, share ideas and read more about any aspect of ministry around life events. This site is the first port of call, and is now used by other departments in Church House, including Vocations.

The information is accessed through each of the life events – weddings, funerals, baptism – and then there are sections in common, with some unique to particular events.

- **Explore the thinking** – gives insights into the background to the research, explains some of the key findings and the reason behind the images, words and resources offered.
- **Downloads** – access useful and important documents, including fees table, new liturgies, logos and other useful handouts.
- **Occasions for follow-up** (baptism) – information about opportunities during the church year that are ideal for families and children, including Godparents' Sunday, Christmas, Easter and many more practical suggestions with prayers, service outlines and ideas.
- **Articles** – a place for in-depth thinking about related issues, longer pieces exploring or explaining ideas, offering advice or introducing new approaches and theological thinking. It is easy to submit an article, which might reflect a piece of independent research or a particular parish practice.
- **Ideas** – lots of useful ideas contributed by parishes across the country who want to share things that work well so that others can benefit. Easy to submit an idea, including photos or PDFs for others to use. A great place for last-minute inspiration!
- There is also information on the site about forthcoming conferences, training events, relevant press stories and a place to ask questions.
- *Church Support Hub Newsletter* – You can sign up here for this regular newsletter which has updates on events, announcements, ideas to help in parish ministry and much more.

www.churchprinthub.org

There is a fantastic range of print resources to support parishes in wedding, funeral and baptism ministry. These can easily be accessed through the Church Print Hub, an online shop where you can choose and order the resources that are available. These include information leaflets, congratulation cards, invitations, address labels, special packs for wedding couples and much more.

- You can customize many of the resources with your church details, service details and other relevant information at no extra charge.
- You can pay with either a card or be invoiced to the parish.
- Products are usually delivered within five working days.

www.pastoralservicesdiary.org

This is a free online administrative tool to manage your life event services, stay in touch with those involved, and receive reminder emails when it's time to use the associated print resources. It helps you to keep in touch regularly and consistently with large numbers of people, sending the right information to the right people at the right moment.

- Enter information appropriate for each life event, including godparents, family members, name of funeral director.
- Add the details of the service as needed.
- Add which minister will be taking the service.
- Add which church will be holding the service in multi-parish benefices.
- Add an estimate of number of guests.
- Manage payments for weddings.
- Print out information as register for weddings.
- Print address labels to do specific mailings for identified groups.
- Plus much more.

It is simple to set up and use. There is full back-up and technical support with queries answered within 48 hours.